Smart Museum of Art
The University of Chicago

Contents

Director's Foreword

Samson Young reconfigures his training as a composer to bring to the fore the sounds that structure and sometimes order daily life. For *Silver moon or golden star, which will you buy of me?*, his first solo exhibition at a museum in the United States, Young has taken the idealism displayed at the 1933 world's fair in Chicago as a point of departure. Obliquely considering the sites and sounds produced by and contained within the automobile, the shopping mall, and the home, the exhibition urgently asks how people adapt to societal changes they have little control over.

Silver moon or golden star demonstrates the singular type of exhibition that can only come to life at a university art museum and represents the unique interdisciplinarity and rigorous research that defines the University of Chicago. The exhibition is the culmination of a research project undertaken by Young during a residency co-sponsored by the University of Chicago's Smart Museum of Art and Neubauer Collegium for Culture and Society. In a truly University-wide endeavor, colleagues generously met with Young to help inform his research as it took shape. Just in the last year, the project was presented in various formats, among them an Object Roundtable at the University's Special Collections Research Center, organized by the Smart Museum's Feitler Center for Academic Inquiry, and a Scholars Roundtable, sponsored by and hosted at The Hong Kong Jockey Club University of Chicago Academic Complex | The University of Chicago Francis and Rose Yuen Campus in Hong Kong. This project highlights the extraordinary potential of a university art museum to reach across departments in cultivating the most innovative art practices around the world.

Beyond the University, the exhibition has inspired the support and unprecedented enthusiasm of organizations from Chicago to Hong Kong. I am honored that we have been able to partner with the Chicago Symphony Orchestra to produce a musical program related to the exhibition, and the Asia Society Hong Kong and EXPO Chicago to organize panel discussions for the exhibition. These partnerships are a testament to Young's remarkable practice and the transnational and interdisciplinary connections it provokes, and they demonstrate the reach of his work in engaging the broadest audience possible.

First and foremost, I would like to thank Samson Young for generously thinking and researching with us at the University of Chicago, and for transforming this research into a wondrous exhibition. I am grateful to Orianna Cacchione, Curator of Global Contemporary Art, who initiated this project and keenly reached out to the University's many centers and departments both here in Chicago and abroad to help Young accomplish the fullest realization of his vision. I am convinced that only at the University of Chicago could this kind of exhibition be achieved, and I am grateful to my colleagues across campus who supported *Silver moon or golden star* from its very earliest conceptions, especially Bala Srinivasan, Executive Vice President for Science, Innovation, and Strategy; David J. Levin, Senior Advisor to the Provost for Arts; Jonathan Lear, Roman Family Director, and Elspeth Carruthers, Executive Director, Neubauer Collegium for Culture and Society; and Bill Michel, Associate Provost and Executive Director, UChicago Arts.

Finally, I am grateful to the generous supporters of this exhibition and the Smart Museum at large for enabling us to accomplish deeply significant exhibitions such as this one. I would like to recognize the collectors from around the world who have generously lent artworks for this exhibition. I want to express my sincere gratitude to the Smart Museum's Board of Governors, especially Gay-Young Cho, Lawrence Chu, and Mirja Haffner, who have championed the museum's ambitious program of global contemporary art in general and this exhibition in particular. The exhibition *Silver moon or golden star* truly represents the Smart Museum's commitment to open the world through the arts and ideas. I am thrilled to welcome visitors to listen to Samson Young's compositions of progress and utopia.

Alison Gass

Dana Feitler Director
Smart Museum of Art

Acknowledgments

003

I have been honored to collaborate with Samson Young over the last two years, traveling down a rabbit hole of songs, theories, and utopias as Samson has developed *Silver moon or golden star, which will you buy of me?* When Samson and I first considered working together, I couldn't have imagined the exhibition's final form, and I have been amazed and grateful for the full support of the Smart Museum of Art and the University of Chicago at large in bringing his vision to life. Samson's practice is deeply engaged in rigorous research, and his work is uniquely suited to be presented at a university art museum. The University provided time, space, and extensive resources, allowing the project to incubate, develop, and transform before my ears and eyes. I have always enjoyed watching Samson's thought process unfold, first through his residency at the Neubauer Collegium for Culture and Society, then over his many research trips to Chicago, my visits to Hong Kong, and three days of filming at the Indiana Dunes State Park.

We are extremely grateful for the resources that our colleagues at the University of Chicago have provided to the project since its nascent stages. In particular, we are grateful to the Neubauer Collegium for co-sponsoring Samson's residency during the fall of 2018. Jonathan Lear, Elspeth Carruthers, Dieter Roelstraete, and Carolyn Ownbey were extremely generous with their time during the preparations for Samson's visit, throughout his residency, and beyond. We have been extremely fortunate for all of the support provided by the University of Chicago Library, and especially by Catherine Uecker, Scott Landvatter, and Jiaxun Benjamin Wu. We are particularly indebted to the Special Collections Research Center, which hosted an Object Roundtable to support the early stages of the exhibition's development. Several members of the University of Chicago's faculty were also incredibly generous in sharing their expertise with Samson during his research. Augusta Read Thomas, Sam Pluta, and Seth Brodsky took the time to meet with Samson, and we are grateful to them for welcoming Samson to engage in the University's intellectual community and for sharing with him their knowledge of the University and their fields. We greatly appreciate the University's leadership, who have advocated and supported this exhibition, especially David J. Levin, Bala Srinivasan, and Bill Michel.

We are also exceedingly grateful for the support of a Provost's Global Faculty Award, which allowed us to host a Scholars Roundtable in Hong

Kong and a panel discussion at the Asia Society about architecture and utopia. The Hong Kong Jockey Club University of Chicago Academic Complex | The University of Chicago Francis and Rose Yuen Campus in Hong Kong welcomed us, and their team aptly managed logistics and facilitated these events in Hong Kong. Special thanks are due to Kitty Chong, Angela Sui, and Chris Hui. Lisa Schrenk, Cole Roskum, and Yang Yueng generously and freely participated in the roundtable, sharing their knowledge of design, fair culture, and progress.

This exhibition has been greatly augmented by a series of public events organized in partnership with institutions here in Chicago and abroad. It has been a tremendous pleasure to work with Stephanie Cristello and the entire EXPO Chicago team to organize a panel discussion at EXPO Chicago's 2019 Symposium. Stephanie graciously initiated discussions that led to the Smart Museum's groundbreaking partnership with the Chicago Symphony Orchestra in hosting the event "World Fair Music." Erika Knierim and the Chicago Symphony Orchestra's Overture Council provided unwavering enthusiasm and led this partnership. I am thankful for their support and for the musicians and choir members who participated in the event. I am also grateful for Avery Trufleman's willingness to join our conversation for the Symposium.

The catalogue reflects the rigorous academic inquiry that has gone into the exhibition, and we are grateful to the authors for their highly original contributions. G Doug Barrett's essay astutely frames Samson's work within the context of critical music and musical contemporary art. Seth Kim-Cohen's thoughtful interview with Samson addresses this project and his practice at large. It has been a tremendous pleasure to work with the catalogue's production team. Joseph Yiu at MAJO Design in Hong Kong has creatively translated the ever-unfolding vision Samson had for the catalogue onto the printed page. This publication could not have been created without the essential leadership of our catalogue manager, Elizabeth Levy, and the exacting hand of our editor, Deirdre O'Dwyer, and proofreader, Natalie Haddad. Their attention to detail and scheduling helped move this volume along in the most efficient of ways. Special recognition is due to Gail Ana Gomez, the Museum's Exhibitions and Publications Coordinator, who worked tirelessly to make sure the book was printed on time to arrive in Chicago for the exhibition's opening.

005

Silver moon or golden star would not have been possible without the generous support of its lenders. These collectors, including William Lim and Tommy Lo, enthusiastically lent their works to the exhibition. The Special Collections Research Center at the University of Chicago Library and Rare Books and Special Collections at the University of British Columbia readily agreed to lend the materials Samson selected from their collections to the exhibition. Edouard Malingue and the team at his gallery in Hong Kong were incredibly generous in facilitating the loan of many drawings. Edouard and Regina Fiorito at Galerie Gisela Capitain in Cologne have provided steadfast support to Samson and his practice in countless ways. We are especially appreciative of Samson's studio team, Vvzela Qu and Lily Yi Yi Chan, for their careful attention in gathering the exhibition's gamut of materials and for coordinating loans from Samson's studio. In addition to these present colleagues at the studio, Samson thanks all who have worked on this project at various points, and without whom a project of this scope would not have been possible, including Christie Wong, Teeda Lee, Andrew Crowe, and Cayn Borthwick.

This extraordinary exhibition has been generously supported by the Smart Museum's Board of Governors, including lead sponsors Gay-Young Cho and Christopher Chiu, Lawrence Chu, and Mirja and Ted Haffner, and event sponsor Bob Buford. I am exceedingly grateful not only for their continued support of contemporary global art at the Smart Museum, but for the many conversations I've had with each about the state of art making in the world today and the urgent call to present it within the confines of the museum.

The Smart Museum commissioned the work *Houses of Tomorrow* (2019) for this exhibition and organized its filming at extant model homes from the 1933 Chicago world's fair, now located in the Indiana Dunes State Park. We are indebted to Todd Zeiger, Director of the Northern Regional Office for Indiana Landmarks, who helped facilitate all aspects of filming. Special thanks are due to Christoph and Charlotte Lichtenfeld, the current custodians of the Armco-Ferro House, who graciously allowed us to film in their summer home. We are exceedingly grateful to Michael Schiefel, a longtime collaborator with Samson; Michael traveled from Hong Kong and braved Indiana's frigid February weather to contribute his vocal talent. Ben Kolak and Stephen Garrett from the Scrappers Film Group were an exceptional crew to work with.

Jonathan Loïc Rogers actively documented the filming, capturing the work in the process of its making. We are also grateful to the Field Museum, Chicago, which generously provided access to their collection of Malvina Hoffman's *Races of Mankind* busts.

I am exceedingly grateful to my colleagues at the Smart Museum, most especially the Dana Feitler Director, Alison Gass, who has championed *Silver moon or golden star* since its inception. Most, if not all, of the Smart Museum's exceptional staff have had a hand in this project. Deputy Directors Michael Christiano and Issa Lampe, with their respective Public Practice and Feitler Center for Academic Inquiry teams, creatively developed the programming around the exhibition. From the first Object Roundtable to the final performance event, Erik L. Peterson, Jason Pallas, Berit Ness, and Natasha Ritsma let their imaginations run loose, greatly augmenting the exhibition's breadth. The exhibition would not have been possible without the dedication and attention to detail of the museum's exhibitions team, led by Deputy Director Jill Sterrett. Sara Hindmarch carefully managed the exhibition's registration, while Ray Klemchuk oversaw its installation and expertly managed all production details. Special recognition is due to Jason Stec, who consulted on the video and audio specifications for the exhibition, ensuring that all looks and sounds exactly as Samson had envisioned. It has been and is always a tremendous honor to work with Gail Ana Gomez, who led the coordination of the exhibition and catalogue. Without her continued support, this exhibition would not have been possible. I would also like to thank my interns, Jasmin Leung, Kaitlyn Spina, and especially Simone Levine, who dutifully researched this exhibition, worked with Samson, and drafted too many documents to count. I am grateful for the crucial support of the Smart's Development team, including former Director of Development Molly McKenzie, Martha Burson, Sara Arnas, Heather Tamburo, and Stephanie Oberhausen. C.J. Lind and Florie Hutchinson have worked diligently to promote the exhibition. This has truly been a team effort, and I am honored to work with such amazing colleagues.

With my deepest gratitude,

Orianna Cacchione

Curator of Global Contemporary Art
Smart Museum of Art

Samson Young: Silver moon or golden star, which will you buy of me?

Orianna Cacchione

Little one, I have dreams to sell,
What will your purchase be?
Will you buy dreams of Fairyland,
Beautiful dreams from me?
Beautiful dreams from me?
Which will you buy?
Which will you buy?
Dreams.
Which will you buy of me?

—A. H. Hyatt, "The Dream-seller"

Then my One World, my ren *(仁), can extend* [only]
to [this] *earth. Can it deliver all of the stars?*

—Kang Youwei[1]

In the early twentieth century, Kang Youwei (1858–1927), a singular figure among Chinese intellectuals, developed a theory of "One World." Kang was, perhaps, China's first utopian thinker, and his impact on intellectuals and reformers was described by one of his students as "a mighty volcanic eruption and huge earthquake."[2] His vision for a single, global community was rooted in the Confucian principle of *ren* (仁, variously translated as benevolence, kindness, humanity, or humanness), which he argued provides a basic and universal experience for all peoples, regardless of geographic location or racial difference. From this perspective, Kang called for equality for all and the dissolution of national borders.

At the time, the term *utopia* was recognized as a so-called Western concept without a formal antecedent in Chinese thought, although ideal societies and places do exist in Confucian, Buddhist, and Taoist literature. The British philosopher Thomas More coined the term in 1516 to name the fictional island described in his treatise *Utopia*, punning on the Greek *eutopia* (good place) and *outopia* (no place). In Europe and the United States during Kang's lifetime, in the context of intense social change brought on by the pace of the industrial revolution and modernity, the concept of utopia denoted a "desire for a different, better way of being."[3] Kang was a reformist and his vision of the promise of a radically transformed and improved life was similarly provoked out of dissatisfaction—with the fall of the Qing Dynasty, the adoption of science and technology from abroad, and the start of the Chinese Civil War.

Today, utopia provides a similar escape—a counterpoint to the neoliberal economy and the new world order—and this thread runs throughout Samson Young's exhibition *Silver moon or golden star, which will you buy of me?* At the core of the exhibition are three music videos that collectively form a song cycle Young calls the Utopia Trilogy (2018–19)—an EP, if you will, that extends into the dystopian, retrotopian, and heterotopian—followed by a fourth video, *The world falls apart into facts #2 (The Dream Seller by E. Markham Lee as performed by the Chinese University of Hong Kong Chorus)* (2019), that documents the surreal performance of a song about dreamscapes being bought and sold. The immersive animations and installations of *Silver moon or golden star* take up the suggestion of recent scholars that rather than thinking about how utopia might be organized, we should instead consider how it is felt.[4] No longer an ideal that is not present, that can only be striven toward, utopia is something that can be experienced affectively, in "small incremental moments" provided by collective performative events.[5] If utopia is an invention of the imagination that can be thought, felt, and experienced, Young's work asks, what is its sound?

Sounding the Everyday, Sounding Power

Young's work, in the simplest of terms, makes audible the sounds that envelope, order, and structure daily life. He remixes and recomposes famous songs heard over and over again on the radio, quotidian noises rarely noticed, unintentional or overlooked melodies, and even sounds that don't yet exist. In making these tones and textures strange, Young brings our attention to them, allowing us to simultaneously hear power and mute it. His compositions are playful considerations of cultural politics, the ethics of musical appropriation, and sound as a metaphor for cultural resonance and resistance. Sound emerges from the background as an experience that subliminally shapes and controls our daily lives, and yet is joyous, hopeful, and sometimes euphoric.

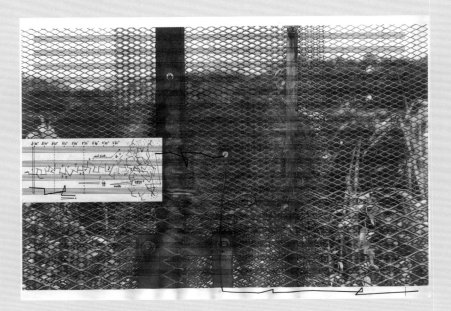

fig. 1
Liquid Borders I (Tsim Bei Tsui & Sha Tau Kok), 2012. Ink, pencil, watercolor, and Xerox print on paper, 17 x 12 1/2 in. (43 x 32 cm). Living Collection, Hong Kong

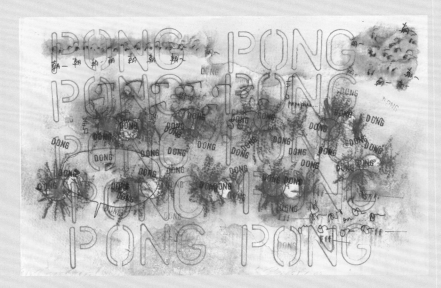

fig. 2
Landschaft (at a garden to the side of the Rouen Cathedral, France, Aug 22, 5:00–5:45 pm), from *For Whom the Bell Tolls* project, 2015. Ink, pencil, and watercolor on paper, 10 7/8 x 7 1/4 in. (27.5 x 18.6 cm). Collection of Ethel Ozen, London

Making visible what might be too complex for the ear to hear fully, Young's earliest sound drawings deconstruct sound as a device that shapes geographical space. For *Liquid Borders* (2012–14) (fig. 1), Young walked along the fenced separation of Hong Kong and mainland China, recording audio and transcribing it into drawings. As graphical notations, these "soundscape sketches" map noises demarcating, or permeating, a boundary. *For Whom the Bell Tolls* (2015) (fig. 2) considers the historical significance of certain bells, and how the reach of a bell's sound could define territorial boundaries. For two months, Young traveled around the world ringing and listening to bells, recording their sounds, and interviewing their current custodians as well as contemporary bell makers. Young's research captures how the sounds of bells are entangled with particularities of place, religion, cultural identity, and politics.

For Young, a bell is like an explosion: a type of sound overload. The politics and violence of such powerful sounds are an important facet of his practice. The performance *Nocturne* (2015) (fig. 3) recreated the sounds of night bombings in the Middle East as aired on broadcast television: Young edited found footage from YouTube into a silent video—or score— for a Foley artist to produce live sound effects using a drum set and household items including rice, tea leaves, and Tupperware. This terrorizing soundtrack could be accessed by the work's audience through its transmission to portable FM radios, available to carry throughout the exhibition space. The next year, Young shifted from making

fig. 3
Installation view of *Pastoral Music*, Team Gallery, New York, 2015, with Young performing *Nocturne*, 2015, sound performance

the story proves not to be true, its appeal incriminates a form of armchair charity as misplaced and merely aspirational. Young's installation at the Hong Kong Pavilion connected different time periods and historical figures through songs emitted from a multichannel speaker system in an uncanny living room overlaid with screens (fig. 6). The soundtrack, props, and onscreen animations strung together disparate places and times— London, North Dakota, and South Africa in the 1980s; Los Angeles in 1985; Hong Kong in 1991; and Moscow in 1957—formulating a new model for exploring tectonic transnational shifts. Included within the presentation was *Young's Muted Situation #21* (2017) (fig. 7), a video featuring members of the Kwan Sing Choir, a "workers club" at the Hong Kong Federation of Trade Unions, whispering the lyrics to Michael Jackson and Lionel Richie's iconic "We Are the World" (1985). In modifying the ensemble (swapping out the original assembly of celebrities) and modulating the song's delivery, Young recast the philanthropic image of the original performance to uncover the economies backing its message. Obliquely, Young's journeying between times and places suggests alternative global histories and recalls Kang Youwei's One World theory, founded on the universal humanity of international peoples.

In recent years, Young has collaborated with Next Generation Sound Synthesis (NESS), a project at the University of Edinburgh in Scotland that produces computer software for the generation of "synthetic" sound. Using NESS-designed programs, he has modeled plans for physics-defying instruments—a twenty-foot-long trumpet, a football-field-sized bugle to be played by a dragon with fire breath (300 degrees Celsius). The resulting series, *Possible Music* (2018) (fig. 8), marks a turn in Young's practice, from calling attention to sounds to inventing them.

All Roads Lead to Chicago, circa 1933

Young's exhibition *Silver moon or golden star* dwells on the 1933 Chicago world's fair (fig. 9), and also passes through the Chinese diaspora, Republican China, the Great Depression, Hong Kong shopping malls, and future highways. Combining the register of the music video—represented in the recent Utopia Trilogy, around which the exhibition is structured—with archival materials, sound drawings, and 3D-printed sculptures, Young animates cacophonous dreamscapes of seemingly divergent and disparate themes, historical events, and

fig. 6
Installation view of *Songs for Disaster Relief*, Hong Kong Pavilion, Fifty-Seventh Venice
Biennale, 2017, with *Palazzo Gundane (homage to the myth-maker who fell to earth)*,
2017, ten-channel sound installation, video, silk-screen on LP covers, ink on vinyl LPs,
3D-printed nylon sculpture, vitrine of found objects, movable curtain system, neon. M+,
Hong Kong

fig. 7
Video still from of *We Are the World*, as performed by the Hong Kong Federation of Trade
Unions Choir *(Muted Situation #21)*, 2017. Eight-channel sound installation, single-
channel high-definition video, 5:26 min.; carpet, ten vintage theater chairs, acoustic
panels, spotlight

015

fig. 8
Video still from *Possible Music #1 (feat. NESS & Shane Aspegren)*, 2018. Eleven-channel sound installation, video with sound, 63 min. Solomon R. Guggenheim Museum, New York

fig. 9
Cover of the brochure *All Roads Lead to Chicago*, published by the Century of Progress International Exposition, Chicago, 1933–34

musicalities. In each video, a central male character spirals out of control—running, floating, multiplying, and falling as he attempts to navigate oddly placeless worlds that morph as they offer objects and ideals both enticing and dangerous. Each music video is set in a different space of the everyday—the car, the store, the home—made possible by modernity's, and then neoliberal capitalism's, promotion of consumerism.

Consumerist fantasies were everywhere in evidence at the 1933 world's fair, where multinational exhibitions proclaimed the motto "Science finds, industry applies, man confirms." The fair's title, "A Century of Progress," advocated optimism just four years after the crash of the US stock market, not long after the First World War, and in the same year that President Franklin D. Roosevelt initiated the New Deal. Indeed, the 1933 edition's promotion of the economy provided a model for the next decade-plus of world's fairs and signified a larger shift in international fair culture and diplomacy, from national pavilions to corporate showcases. National pavilions reinforcing imperialism had comprised the original European expositions, but during the cross-Atlantic recession many governments could not afford to mount such displays. American corporations stepped in to display not only goods but the very production processes used to make them, including working assembly lines (figs. 10, 11). Dioramas, murals, moving images, and didactic texts attempted to humanize new industries and ways of life, and they encouraged public spending as a remedy to an economy supposedly weakened by underconsumption.[9] Reflecting a move in the US financial system from a model based on land acquisition and individual entrepreneurship to corporate accumulation, the increasing complexity of consumer culture tacitly anticipated a new world order, wherein a distinctly American form idealism would prevail.[10]

fig. 10
Postcard of "The Kraft Mayonnaise Kitchen—The Bottling, Jar Capping, and Labeling Machine," Century of Progress International Exposition, Chicago, 1933–34

fig. 11
Postcard of "Chevrolet's Automobile Assembly Line—General Motors Building," Century of Progress International Exposition, Chicago, 1933–34

Thousands of cars delivered visitors to a fair that aggressively marketed the automobile as an example of scientific progress and modern convenience. In advertisements and popular culture, the car had become synonymous with freedom and unprecedented mobility, yet cars were still dangerous, loud machines that needed to be regulated and engineered; "mass adoption created mass chaos that threatened everyone's safety," and necessitated driver-safety campaigns.[11] Young's first music video, *The highway is like a lion's mouth* (2018) offers a safety jingle that emphasizes the car as both symbol of optimism and source of anxiety, mixing various and incessant safety directions— "mobile off, seatbelt on," "look left, look right," "aware today, alive tomorrow." From the "horseless carriage" of the early twentieth century to the dawn of driverless personal transport, cars have promised development and also posed a physical threat and facilitated forms of political control. The video's central character is constantly on the verge of being pulled apart as he navigates driving through obstacles in a video game landscape of race tracks and monopoly boards. He speeds across the recently opened sea bridge connecting Hong Kong to Macau and mainland China—an engineering feat that is more political symbol of mainland China's administrative control over the Special Administrative Regions than practical thoroughfare.[12]

Around the perimeter of *The highway*'s installation, robotized "lemons," in the work *Line follower* (2019), drive along a prescribed black path, as defective cars might in a fully automated future. *The highway* is also accompanied by a series of drawings, *My car makes noises* (2018), that visualize the actual sounds cars make due to safety technologies, including those designed to effect a sense of security—for example, the hard thud of a car door as it closes. The drawings also playfully record the sounds people make to describe how their cars are in need of repair; these seemingly disparate references are echoed in *The highway*, which concludes with a warning: "You don't own the road."

From the automobile, Young shifts his focus for the next music video to the shopping mall (which the automobile's large-scale adoption made possible in North America). *Da Da Company* (2019) juxtaposes utopian notions from both sides of the Pacific, placing Won Alexander Cumyow— an acolyte of Kang Youwei born in 1861 in British Columbia, present- day Canada—in a consumerist disaster scenario set to a soundtrack that reconfigures the beloved Rodgers and Hammerstein show tune "My Favorite Things" (1959). The Chinese-Canadian is entranced in an 1980s-era mall as he frantically attempts to secure the return of the emperor to Peking.[13] Young stages nostalgic longing as a retrotopian impulse in *Da Da Company*, where the future exists as a restoration of "a vaguely remembered past," to borrow a phrase from theorist Zygmunt Bauman.[14] Won's reconstructionist tendencies are allegorized in Young's animation of a construction worker futilely pushing against falling water in the soon-flooded mall, where dynastic antiques and trash alike float by as the debris of overconsumption; meanwhile, the mood of nostalgic reverie persists, enhanced by interspersed clips of arcade games, the 1988 Chinese television documentary *Heshang* (River Elegy), and the 1994 Taiwanese movie *Eat Drink Man Woman*.

Da Da Company is situated, in *Silver moon or golden star*, within Young's staging of a rundown storeroom, complete with dropped ceiling and outmoded office chairs, in which hang his series of photographs *City Garden* (2019). These images capture the current incarnation of the shopping mall near Young's childhood home in Hong Kong that once housed a Da Da Company department store. Over time, the mall's occupants have changed from retail and commercial shops to "cram schools" and storefront churches. The music video ends sharply with static-laced footage of a 1980s television commercial enticing Hong Kong viewers to move to Singapore; its insidious refrain—"It's a heaven over there"—suggests that mainland China's narrative of reconstruction might not provide its promised benefits.

Returning to Chicago and 1933, the Utopia Trilogy's third video, *Houses of Tomorrow* (2019), is set in two model homes constructed at the world's fair to advertise the modern American dream, centered on the home "as the primary engine for consumerism."[15] The newest consumer appliances, foods, and building construction were highlighted in the Armco-Ferro House, which Young shows restored to its original early 1930s splendor. The second model home, architect George Fred Keck's House of Tomorrow—a *machine à habiter* (machine for living)—once demonstrated an efficiency that "entirely upset the conventional ideas of a home" (fig. 12).[16] In Young's reimagining of modern domestic life, Keck's structure is vacant and stripped to the studs—laying bare the physical deterioration of this particular vision of the future.

fig. 12
Exterior view of George Fred Keck's House of Tomorrow, Century of Progress
International Exposition, Chicago, 1933–34

Houses of Tomorrow revisits a specifically American vein of progressive thinking, its degeneration, and how it has been exported around the world. As the music video follows a lone performer singing "Did You Ever See a Dream Walking?"—a Bing Crosby hit in 1933—international forces persistently interject into a conventional vision of American domesticity, including a creeping Chinese Nationalist (Kuomintang) soldier. In 1933, the Nationalist (Kuomintang) government in China was under attack by both the insurgent Communist party and Japanese forces (then occupying Manchuria). While political disarray and social upheaval foreclosed the possibility that the Chinese government might organize a pavilion for Chicago, China was nonetheless represented by a privately sponsored Chinese-style courtyard pavilion, a reconstructed Buddhist shrine, and a display on the railroad in Japanese Manchuria. Translated into Chinese as *wanguo bolanhui* (萬國博覽會, "ten thousand nations' exhibitions"), world's fairs represented coerced multinational engagement and constituted an aspect of the country's modernization.[17] Set within this literal "political theater, " the third music video draws out not only these stately international relations but also the essentialist theories of race, culture, class, and hygiene that informed them. Animated within *Houses of Tomorrow* are busts sculpted by Malvina Hoffman for the *Races of Mankind* exhibition at the Field

fig. 13
Installation view of Malvina Hoffman's sculptures in *The Races of Mankind* exhibition hall,
Field Museum, Chicago, 1933

Museum in Chicago (fig. 13), which opened during the fair. Eventually, Young burns it all down, setting the houses ablaze in the video.

A fourth, nonanimated video accompanies the Utopia Trilogy in *Silver moon or golden star*. Titled *The world falls apart into facts #2 (The Dream Seller by E. Markham Lee as performed by the Chinese University of Hong Kong Chorus),* it documents a performance of the song "The Dream-seller" (1904; music by E. Markham Lee, lyrics by A. H. Hyatt). This final tune, sung by the student chorus of the Chinese University of Hong Kong, combines capitalist desire with orientalist fantasy to imagine, in Young's description, "a cow's dream of a horse."[18] As with the other musical numbers playing throughout the exhibition, sonic manipulations render the song disorienting. Young's interpretation of "The Dream-seller"—music traditionally arranged for a children's choir— once heard is both familiar and strange.

From Houses of Tomorrow to the World of Tomorrow
The 1933 world's fair in Chicago was among the first to market utopia as a future for ready consumption. Six years after the Chicago fair, New York hosted another version of the international exposition, titled "The World of Tomorrow" (1939–40). On its grounds, Salvador Dalí

fig. 14
Installation view of Salvador Dalí's "Dream of Venus" pavilion, New York
World's Fair, 1939–40

staged a pavilion, the "Dream of Venus," that beckoned visitors into a dreamworld gone surrealist, to be entered by passing through a giant pair of legs. Inside the fun house were two swimming pools with live, scantily clad women gliding past a landscape of mermaids, dancing lobsters, and other signifiers of the libidinous imaginary (fig. 14). It appeared as a hedonistic transgression at a fair otherwise espousing the idealist and progressive vision of a budding consumer consciousness—"selling not just a genuine vision of utopia that could come about in the next two decades but also commercial products and mass entertainment."[19]

Like Dalí's unexpected pavilion, Young's Utopia Trilogy transports the viewer through a series of immersive spaces. Each music video turns on its head a familiar genre of song: the safety jingle, which in *The highway* transforms the protection and freedom of the automobile into an anxiety-inducing reminder of 24-7 vigilance; the show tune, which in *Da Da Company* cautions against longing for the foregone, or for the future as recklessly promised in glitzy advertising; and finally, the radio hit, which leads to the House of Tomorrow seen burning, suggesting just how tenuous dreams of an ideal future are. Young's music videos warn against falling prey to the taunt of the chorus in the "The Dream-seller"—"Silver moon or golden star, which will you buy of me?" Utopia cannot be bought and sold; instead, as Young observes, optimism needs to be paid attention to and carefully maintained.

NOTES

1   Kang Youwei, *Ta T'ung Shu: The One-World Philosophy of K'ang Yu-wei*, trans. Laurence G. Thompson (London: George Allen & Unwin, 1958), 80.

2   Liang Qichao, quoted in Kung-chuan Hsiao, "In and Out of Utopia: K'ang Yu-wei's Social Thought," *Chung Chi Journal* 7, no. 2 (May 1968): 101.

3   Ruth Levitas, quoted in Howard P. Segal, *Utopias: A Brief History from Ancient Writings to Virtual Communities* (Malden, MA: Wiley-Blackwell, 2012), 7.

4   See Rachel Bowditch and Pegge Vissicaro, introduction to *Performing Utopia*, ed. Rachel Bowditch and Pegge Vissicaro (Chicago: University of Chicago Press, 2016), 1.

5   Jill Dolan, "Performance, Utopia, and the 'Utopian Performative,'" *Theatre Journal* 53, no. 3 (October 2001): 460.

6   Samson Young, "Muted Situation #1: Muted String Quartet," 2014, artist's website, https://www.thismusicisfalse. com/#/the-anatomy-of-a-string-quartet/.

7   Anthony Leung Po-shan, "Yellow in C Major—Samson Young's Perceptual Cutting," in *Samson Young: Songs for Disaster Relief, Hong Kong in Venice (A Mixtape)*, ed. Ying Kwok and Sonia So (West Kowloon Cultural District, Hong Kong: M+, 2017), 37.

8   Doryun Chong, "Introduction: Failed Aspiration," in *Samson Young: Songs for Disaster Relief, Hong Kong in Venice (A Mixtape)*, 16.

9   See Lisa Schrenk, *Building a Century of Progress: The Architecture of Chicago's 1933–34 World's Fair* (Minneapolis: University of Minnesota Press, 2007), 27.

10 Ibid., 20.

11 Sarah A. Seo, *Policing the Open Road: How Cars Transformed American Freedom* (Cambridge, MA: Harvard University Press, 2019), 12.

12 "'It is very odd. It crosses that much of the sea, and yet ordinary people cannot use it. What's the point of that?' said Claudia Mo, a pro-democracy lawmaker in Hong Kong. 'This project is so obviously a political symbol. I'm sure Beijing knew clearly that we didn't quite need it and that it was not necessary for the time being.'" Quoted in Shibani Mahtani, "The world's longest bridge-tunnel brings China even closer to Hong Kong. Not everyone is pleased," *Washington Post*, October 23, 2018, https://www.washingtonpost.com/world/asia_pacific/china-just-opened-the-worlds-longest-bridge-tunnel-hong-kong-critics-wish-it-never-was-built/2018/10/23/bf05e6c2-d6a3-11e8-9559-712cbf726d1c_story.html?utm_term=.ef0831dc33e0.

13 At the time, China was struggling to reaffirm and also modernize its national identity after losing territory to foreign powers, especially the Japanese in the first Sino-Japanese War, leading to an intellectual movement for self-strengthening. While living in exile in Canada, Kang Youwei founded the Society to Preserve the Emperor, petitioning for the reestablishment the Qing Emperor.

14 Zygmunt Bauman, *Retrotopia* (Cambridge, UK; Malden, MA: Polity Press, 2017), 6. Bauman connects retroutopianism to the recent rise of nationalism globally.

15 See Robert W. Rydell, "Making America (More) Modern: American's Depression-Era World's Fairs," introduction to *Designing Tomorrow: America's World's Fairs of the 1930s*, ed. Robert W. Rydell and Laura Burd Schiavo (New Haven, CT: Yale University Press, 2010), 10.

16 Schrenk, *Building a Century of Progress*, 159.

17 Cole Roskam, "Situating Chinese Architecture within 'A Century of Progress': The Chinese Pavilion, the Bendix Golden Temple, and the 1933 Chicago World's Fair," *Journal of the Society of Architectural Historians* 73, no. 3 (September 2014): 347.

18 Conversation with the author, June 2019.

19 Howard P. Segal, *Utopias: A Brief History from Ancient Writings to Virtual Communities* (Chichester, West Sussex, UK: Wiley-Blackwell, 2012), 37.

Unhearing Utopia: Samson Young's Utopia Trilogy as Musical Contemporary Art

G Douglas Barrett

How can a musical art practice engage contemporaneity understood as a fictional and, relatedly, utopian "spatialization" of global capitalism's historical temporality?[1] Samson Young's foray into music video making, the Utopia Trilogy, is a watershed music video song cycle that sets three original works composed by Young and sung by the German musician Michael Schiefel—*The highway is like a lion's mouth* (2018), *Da Da Company* (2019), and *Houses of Tomorrow* (2019)—to imagery that combines 3D animation with text, original and found footage, and screen captures that occasionally reveal the artist's digital production process. *Houses of Tomorrow* gestures to utopia's anticipatory future, while the 3D spaces of *Da Da Company* and *The highway* flatten utopia's suspensive temporality into spatial expanse.

Altogether, the Utopia Trilogy configures a range of historical and cultural references, from low- to highbrow, in the construction of musicalized imaginary space. The first of the videos, *The highway*, takes the form of a road-safety jingle: "Look left, look right, look left, again," Schiefel chants over a low piano-and-synthesizer riff (fig. 1). While it recalls the "share the road" campaigns that emerged in the United States during the motor age of the 1910s to 1930s,[2] *The highway* also draws together an international range of contemporary car and street cultures, whether real or fictive: a partially destroyed Lamborghini drives through a dreamscape racetrack, for instance, while a traditional Chinese lion dance performed in the street meets highway surveillance footage streamed through virtual reality goggles.

The soundtrack of *Da Da Company* recomposes the show tune "My Favorite Things" from Rodgers and Hammerstein's *The Sound of Music* (1959). The familiar melody becomes audible amid noisy viola sounds and a swinging vocal bassline as "sins" are substituted in for "things" and the popular Chinese dish "moo goo gai" for "schnitzel with noodles," among other alterations (fig. 2). *Da Da Company* reworks signifiers of the historical avant-garde via transnational consumer culture: the title's approximation of the Pīnyīn romanization of 大大 (*dà dà*, meaning "big big") refers to the name of a shopping mall in Hong Kong near to where Young grew up the in the 1980s (which the artist compares to those found in North American Chinatowns) and to the early-twentieth-century art movement.[3] The animation follows a male-bodied figurine who dances around floating consumer detritus in an otherwise empty

fig. 1
Video still from *The highway is like a lion's mouth*, 2018

fig. 2
Video still from *Da Da Company*, 2019

shopping interior, while workers repair spewing soda fountains and broken ice cream dispensers.

Houses of Tomorrow (2019)—in many ways the centerpiece of the trilogy—is a cultural and artistic analysis of the world's fair that opened in Chicago in 1933; it revisits Bing Crosby's version, released that same year, of the song "Did You Ever See a Dream Walking?" Acknowledging the international exposition's signature blend of racio-colonial utopian futurism, Young's music video features imagery from the model homes on exhibit and 3D scans of Malvina Hoffman's *Races of Mankind* [4] sculptures (fig. 3), along with promotional materials for Miracle Whip, unveiled for the first time at the fair.

fig. 3
Plaster sculpture of Dr. Hu Shih from eastern China, from Malvina Hoffman's *Races of Mankind project*, 1930s. The Field Museum, Chicago

A tension emerges between the videos' visions of utopia conceived as an ideological investment in the temporality of modernity and a musical version of "the contemporary" that insists on a kind of spatialization of modernity's historical time. Young's interdisciplinary artistic practice confronts such tension by drawing from music yet departing equally from its modernist incarnation as new music and the quasi-medium-specificity of sound art. In this sense, Young's work can be considered an instance of *critical music*—as an artistic practice that uses music as form and subject matter yet operates beyond the medium of sound according to contemporary art's postconceptual and postmedium condition.[5] Such practices often make use of traditional musical forms yet transform them or present them in less conventional contexts. Young's music videos rework the song form while they expand it to address the interrelated space-times of contemporaneity.

Through the trilogy's layering of the contemporary's multiple geopolitical times—its musical representations of consumer culture and inequality across democratic and authoritarian forms of capitalism—the work figures more significantly as an instance of *musical contemporary art*: postformalist musical art practices that engage the contemporary conceived as a spatialization of the historical temporality of global capitalism.[6] These are, foremost, contemporary art practices, yet they use music as site, subject, or form. Rather than simply grafting the concerns of one field onto another, musical contemporary art names the lacuna in knowledge and practice that has arisen, since at least the Second World War, between contemporary art and music. Contemporary art, on the one hand, emerges as a result of the radical transformations of the postwar avant-garde into what Peter Osborne and others have called "postconceptual art": a radically generic art beyond specific mediums, which instead prioritizes discursive meaning and social process. New music, on the other hand, continues to struggle with its formal status as a nonconceptual, sound-based medium of art that inherits its concept from the discourses of aesthetic modernism and absolute music (the nineteenth-century movement that transformed the formerly polyvalent Western concept of music into instrumental sound). Today, phrases such as "contemporary music" or "contemporary composition" are often used to mean "recently composed art music" or as stand-ins for the modernist category of "new music." Rarely, though, are such expressions attached to any kind of world-historical periodizing function or to the concerns of art history. At the same time, sound art, while avoiding some of the tendencies of modern art music, remains anachronistic in that it relies on a quasi-formalist medium-specificity at odds with contemporary art's generic and postconceptual condition.

A coherent body of criticism and theory, moreover, has not accompanied the various recent musical art practices that do use postconceptual strategies to address the contemporary. *Musical contemporary art*, through its application to practices such as Young's, attempts to account for this gap. What counts as musical contemporary art? In short, as music becomes contemporary—that is, as it addresses the contemporary defined as the historical temporality of global capitalism—it also becomes contemporary art. How, then, does Young's work engage the contemporary?

The trilogy assembles a disjunctive network of signifiers that link utopian imaginaries of the twentieth century, with an emphasis on the 1930s, to the historical present. The song cycle indeed highlights a decade many have compared to the present: the coupling of a global economy in crisis with the rise of nationalism and fascism alongside progress myths fueled by technological advance. Fascism and the New Deal, each having offered its own utopian program in the lead-up to the Second World War, return today albeit with the respective modifiers "neo" and, in the US, "Green." *Da Da Company*'s references to *The Sound of Music*, given the latter's plot point around the 1938 Nazi annexation of Austria, invite a comparison to the rise of the far right around the world in recent times. Meanwhile, techniques used in today's green buildings can be traced to architect George Fred Keck's introduction of passive solar energy in his flagship House of Tomorrow at the 1933 world's fair. *The highway*'s invocation of extensive street, roadway, and tunnel development during the Great Depression points to the massive unemployment now heralded with the advent of self-driving cars. Rather than repeating itself, though, history appears as an echo. The uniform-clad Chinese Nationalist government officer in *Houses of Tomorrow* (fig. 4) reminds us that in 1933, as the world's fair was opening in Chicago, the Nationalists achieved a major victory against the Communists in the Chinese Civil War; today, mainland China exercises its continued dominance over the Nationalist Republic of China government, which fled to Taiwan in 1949, in routine military drills over Taipei. The present is distinguished, moreover, by its implementation of an interdependent world economy. Although capitalism has been in some nontrivial sense "global" since at least the latter part of the eighteenth century, "the contemporary" understood as a periodizing concept refers to a postwar era of globalization defined by market deregulation and global finance capital. How, then, does the Utopia Trilogy's comparison of the interwar period and the present relate to the contemporary, especially if the latter is understood as a *post*war periodization?

Here it is important to note that the contemporary does not designate a period thoroughly separate from the modern, but rather attempts to mark the complex temporality of its fractured geopolitical unity— to represent the historical time of global capitalism through the presence of a multiplicity of simultaneous historical presents registered on a planetary scale. The modern can be conceived as

fig. 4
Production documentation of *Houses of Tomorrow*, 2019

the historical production of the temporality of the new, exhibited perhaps most transparently in German with the late-eighteenth-century lexico-historiographical shift from *neue Zeit* (new time) to *Neuzeit* (modernity).[7] As a historical temporality, the contemporary is distinct from the modern, as Osborne contends, yet it "interacts with the temporality of modernity—the differential temporality of the new—in fiendishly complicated ways."[8] The contemporary is no longer governed strictly by modernity's human-directed production of the new, or anthropogenic action; it is no longer *historical* in the sense of future-oriented progress. For Suhail Malik, this means that the contemporary is "posthistorical": although the contemporary arrives as a historical departure from modernity, and is in that sense new, contemporaneity is characterized precisely by its lack of continued historical progress, or the absence of a modernist new.[9] This sense of the contemporary nonetheless resists the kind of vulgar stagism found in the work of both historians and art historians, where one period cleanly replaces another.[10] Alexander Alberro and Terry Smith, for instance, define the contemporary as beginning in 1989 with the triumph of neoliberalism and its heightened inequalities, the integration of electronic and digital culture, and globalization with its production of post- and decolonial subjectivities.[11] Such elements doubtless appear in Young's work, although their continuity with the utopian valences of modernism is also evident—consider, for instance, *Da Da Company*'s appropriation of a 1980s TV advertisement promoting emigration to Singapore, which aired frequently on Hong Kong television in the 1980s and contains the refrain "It's a heaven over there" (fig. 5).

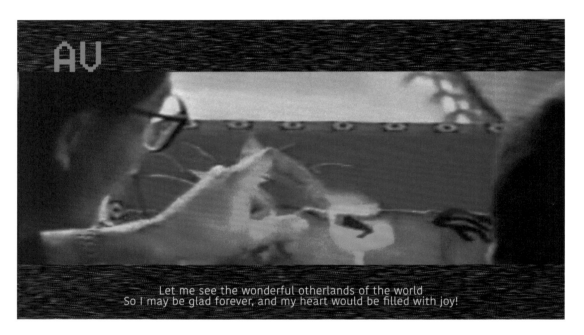

Let me see the wonderful otherlands of the world
So I may be glad forever, and my heart would be filled with joy!

fig. 5
Video still from *Da Da Company*, 2019

If the contemporary stands for the posthistorical spatialization of the time of global capitalism, then utopia represents an ideological investment in the temporality of modernity—which is, preeminently, a *musical* temporality. Utopia, along with the new, composes the very motor of modernity: it operates according to the logic of a resolution-to-come, emblematized in the "not yet."[12] This is a suspension homologous to the buildup before the resolution of a dominant chord to its tonic—felt, for instance, when the Rodgers and Hammerstein melody cited in *Da Da Company* arrives on the word "things." Such a musical-libidinal tension, it seems, wants to resolve, to "progress." But toward what?

Music was, in this sense, the very model for Ernst Bloch's *The Spirit of Utopia*, which the philosopher wrote during the First World War and subsequently published and revised in the years that followed. Rather than the texted song forms to which Young's trilogy refers, though, it was instrumental music—and, more specifically, absolute music— that guided Bloch's thought. (In the sixteenth century, Saint Thomas More imagined texted Renaissance music, which he referred to as *musica reservata*, as integral to his founding concept of utopia.)[13] But not all dissonances resolve harmoniously. Likewise, Bloch insists on the uncertainty of speculation over teleology: "time presses toward an unknown goal, and it is more than likely that in more particular areas of music the same problem of the goal arises objectively that animates the total process of the symphony of history." Such a temporality, no less than the symphony of history, does integrate space through what Bloch refers to as a contrapuntal "horizontalism." Yet even the latter is based on a sense of succession and progression in which utopia's suspensive temporality of the "not yet" remains central. Utopia is the "musical-historical time" of modernity.[14]

As much as time is integral to utopia, the concept is also structured through space, particularly in the interplay between real and fictional space. Recall that More's original model for utopia, a play on the word's Greek connotations as both "good place" and "no place," was an imaginary island in the New World. Unlike its nonfictional counterparts, More's utopia banished private property, yet like them it had slaves. His utopia was real in that it borrowed from existing economic models of colonialism and slavery, yet fictional in its reference to an imagined future state of communal property relations. It wasn't until the nineteenth century that Marx and Engels would propose, beyond the utopian socialists of the eighteenth century, a concrete program for the abolition of the actually existing conditions of the capitalist present in favor of a potentially global state of communism. Rather than the connotations of the English *science* (or, relatedly, the French *la science*) of "scientific socialism," however, it was the broader meaning of the

German *Wissenschaft*—as erudition, learning, and knowledge—that underpinned such a vision.[15]

Nonetheless, many of the recent imaginary spaces of utopia, especially following the fall of the Soviet Union and through the cultural logic of postmodernism, appear as some form of science *fiction*. This accounts perhaps for Fredric Jameson's turn, after the failures of postmodernism, to sci-fi in what he termed utopian studies.[16] But it also accounts for some of the more interesting spatial utopias envisioned by twentieth-century avant-garde and neo-avant-garde movements. Here, *Da Da Company* suggests a comparison with the work of Dutch Situationist architect Constant Nieuwenhuys, for its similar layering of the disparate space-times of modernity. Nieuwenhuys's New Babylon project of the 1960s proposed giant cities that would float seemingly superimposed over fully automated cybernetic factories below, allowing inhabitants lives of pure play (fig. 6).[17] In the 3D spaces of *Da Da Company*, architectural surfaces literally hover over one another and occasionally intersect, as commodities (green tea bottles, broccoli stalks, fruit tarts) glide past workers who endlessly toil amid the protagonist's ludic dancing—a model of the contemporary as such (fig. 7).

fig. 6
Constant Nieuwenhuys, *New Babylon*, 1971. Etching with drypoint, 5 3/4 x 9 1/4 in. (14.5 x 23.6 cm). Collection Fondation Constant

Gods of the free world and rulers in Eden

fig. 7
Video still from *Da Da Company*, 2019

The contemporary is, in this sense, a utopia of pure space: a paradigmatically futureless utopia of flattened time arrived at through a familiar logic. What the modern did with temporality the contemporary does to space: whereas modernity proposed a permanent state of anticipatory suspense from the perspective of a unified place, the contemporary is the speculative, fictional collapsing of a multiplicity of spaces onto a fixed present. As opposed to modernity's temporal horizon of possibility, the contemporary flattens historical movement into static spatiality. This means that the contemporary is also utopian, both in the imaginative act of this performative flattening and its refusal to imagine its own futurity.

The utopian dimension of the contemporary is both positive and negative. According to Osborne, "Negatively, it involves a disavowal; positively, it is an act of the productive imagination. It involves a disavowal—a disavowal of its own futural, speculative basis—to the extent to which it projects an actual conjunction of all present times." He continues, "It is a productive act of imagination to the extent to which it performatively projects a non-existent unity onto the disjunctive relations between coeval times. In this respect, in rendering present the absent time of a unity of times, all constructions of the contemporary are fictional."[18] As a fictional projection of such a hypothetical unity of times, the contemporary rotates, as it were, modernity's temporal utopian axis, turning its suspensive, anticipatory time into the static, futureless space of posthistory. If it is easier to imagine the end of the world than the end of capitalism, that is because the latter speaks the language of a bygone idiom—the utopian musical-historical time of modernity—whereas the former has an actual basis in the evermore proximal environmental constraints on the contemporary: the end of the world has, in many ways, already begun.[19] How, then, can musical contemporary art practices address such an impasse?

Young's trilogy broadens the purview of the contemporary temporally and artistically as it interrogates the utopian premises of modernity and contemporaneity through the construction of musicalized imaginary space. Temporally, it underscores disjunctive continuities between the modernist utopian imaginary during the interwar period and contemporary sites of cultural and political contention. *Da Da Company* and *The highway* point from different perspectives to transnational consumer culture and inequality, while in *Houses of Tomorrow* the Chicago world's fair functions as a historical touchstone that links to the contemporary valences of racism and the environment—which, not incidentally, mirror utopia's early modern conception as a slave-owning society in perfect harmony with nature.[20] Artistically, the Utopia Trilogy extends the field of contemporary art to include music as both content and form. Working against the formalist tenets of new music, Young's postconceptual approach to the song cycle combines various media with references spanning from art music to transnational popular culture.

Rather than incidental, music is integral to Young's interrogation of the problem of utopia, which he traces across the modern and contemporary: his music videos point to the utopianism at play in the contemporary's disavowal of futurity, while it discourages a continued investment in modernity's musical-historical time. It likewise eschews a return to the formalisms of medium or the aesthetic through "sound" and even "listening." As musical contemporary art, the trilogy suggests not simply that we divest from utopia, but that we become aware of its lingering audibility even in the posthistorical present. Hearing utopia only to *un*hear it, Young recomposes the musical space of the contemporary.

NOTES

1   This reading of contemporaneity and the contemporary is taken from Peter Osborne. See Peter Osborne, *The Postconceptual Condition: Critical Essays* (New York: Verso, 2017), loc. 24, 69 of 373.

2   See Peter D. Norton, *Fighting Traffic: The Dawn of the Motor Age in the American City* (Cambridge, MA: MIT Press, 2008).

3   Godfre Leung, ed., *Samson Young: It's a heaven over there* (Vancouver: Centre A, 2019), 3.

4   Hoffman's sculptures remained on display at the Field Museum in Chicago until 1969, at which time they were placed in storage following protests. See Marianne Kinkel, *Races of Mankind: The Sculptures of Malvina Hoffman* (Champaign: University of Illinois Press, 2011); and Linda Kim, *Race Experts: Sculpture, Anthropology, and the American Public in Malvina Hoffman's Races of Mankind* (Lincoln: University of Nebraska Press, 2018).

5   For more on *critical music* and my development of the term, see G Douglas Barrett, *After Sound: Toward a Critical Music* (New York: Bloomsbury, 2016). I consider John Baldessari's 1972 video work *Baldessari Sings LeWitt* as a "song cycle," for instance, because it sets Sol LeWitt's 1969 *Sentences on Conceptual Art* to a series of folk tunes and popular melodies. See ibid., 77–86.

6   See G Douglas Barrett, "Contemporary Art and the Problem of Music: How Contemporary is Contemporary Music?," in "Techniques of Contemporaneity," ed. Patrick Valiquet, special issue, *Contemporary Music Review* (forthcoming).

7   Reinhart Koselleck, *Futures Past: On the Semantics of Historical Time*, trans. Keith Tribe (New York: Columbia University Press, 2004), 224–25. *Neuzeit* broadly refers to the period following the middle ages, but used more specifically it marks the onset of industrialism in the late eighteenth century.

8   Osborne, *The Postconceptual Condition*, 28.

9   Suhail Malik, "Contra-Contemporary," in *The Future of the New*, ed. Thijs Lijster (Amsterdam: Veliz Press, forthcoming). Malik derives his notion of anthropogenic action, in part, from Hannah Arendt, *The Human Condition*, 2nd ed. (1958; Chicago: University of Chicago Press, 1998), 177–78.

10   Osborne, *The Postconceptual Condition*, 28.

11   See Alexander Alberro, response to "Questionnaire on 'The Contemporary,'" *October* 130 (Fall 2009): 55; and Terry Smith, *What is Contemporary Art?* (Chicago: University of Chicago Press, 2009).

12   This phrase originates in Bloch but was substantially taken up by Adorno, especially in his *Hegel: Three Studies* (1963). See Theodor W. Adorno, *Hegel: Three Studies*, trans. Shierry Weber Nicholson (Cambridge, MA: MIT Press, 1993); and Max Blechman, "'Not Yet': Adorno and the Utopia of Conscience," *Cultural Critique* 70 (Fall 2008): 177–98.

13   Nan C. Carpenter, "A Song for All Seasons: Sir Thomas More and Music," *Comparative Literature* 33, no. 2 (Spring 1981): 113–36.

14   Ernst Bloch, *The Spirit of Utopia*, trans. Anthony A. Nassar (1918; Stanford, CA: Stanford University Press, 2000), 130 and 135. See also Bloch's three-volume *The Principle of Hope* (trans. Stephen Plaice, Paul Knight, and Neville Plaice; Cambridge, MA: MIT Press, 1995), originally published between 1954 and 1959.

15   Paul Thomas, *Marxism and Scientific Socialism: From Engels to Althusser* (London: Routledge, 2008), 30.

16   Fredric Jameson, *Archaeologies of the Future: The Desire Called Utopia and Other Science Fiction* (New York: Verso, 2005).

17   See McKenzie Wark, "New Babylon," in *The Beach Beneath the Street: The Everyday Life and Glorious Times of the Situationist International* (New York: Verso, 2011), 135–46.

18   Osborne, *The Postconceptual Condition*, 69. Emphasis removed.

19   Fredric Jameson and Slavoj Žižek each attribute the phrase "It's easier to imagine the end of the world than the end of capitalism" to the other. See Mark Fisher, *Capitalist Realism: Is There No Alternative* (New York: Zero Books, 2009), 1–11.

20   For an ecocritical reading of More's *Utopia*, see Ivo Kamps and Melissa L. Smith, "Utopian Ecocriticism: Naturalizing Nature in Thomas More's Utopia," in *Early Modern Ecostudies: From the Florentine Codex to Shakespeare*, ed. Thomas Hallock, Ivo Kamps, and Karen L. Raber (New York: Palgrave MacMillan, 2008), 115–30.

Messy, Self-Contradictory, Uncomfortable, and Complicated: Samson Young in conversation with Seth Kim-Cohen

In April 2019, during the final planning stages of Silver moon or golden star, which will you buy of me?, *Samson Young spoke with artist-critic Seth Kim-Cohen about his processes in making the works for the exhibition and their installation at the Smart Museum. The following is a condensed version of their conversation.*

Seth Kim-Cohen: Let's start at the top. Can you say something about the title of the exhibition *Silver moon or golden star, which will you buy of me?* And, can you discuss how you generally arrive at titles and how they function in your work?

Samson Young: The title usually—but not always—comes to me in the middle of making an exhibition, when the different pieces are partially completed. *Silver moon or golden star, which will you buy of me?* is from A. H. Hyatt's lyrics for the song "The Dream-seller" (1904), by the English composer E. Markham Lee. It's not an incredibly popular or well-known piece, but one year it was assigned as part of an annual choral music competition organized by the Hong Kong government (then still colonial). The local school I was attending at the time (before I left for further high schooling in Sydney) participated in the competition—I was a member of the choir and that's how I know it. The song is incredibly sweet, but I distinctly remember trying to picture what a "dream-seller" would actually look like, and having a vague image of a sinister-looking character. It's a very specific kind of creepy, because absolutely nothing in the music or even the lyrics alone would suggest it. Right now I'm finishing the last video for the exhibition, *The world falls apart into facts #2 (The Dream Seller by E. Markham Lee as performed by the Chinese University of Hong Kong Chorus)* (2019) (fig. 1), which is a sort of strange performance of the "The Dream-seller." It's not super clear what my approach is going to be yet, but it's going to be about that sort of dissonance between the song itself and the picture of the song in my head.

fig. 1
Production documentation of *The world falls apart into facts #2 (The Dream Seller by E. Markham Lee as performed by the Chinese University of Hong Kong Chorus)*, 2019

SK-C: The term "dream-seller" brings to mind the important theme of utopia in your work, and perhaps a reckoning with failed utopian ambitions. How does this exhibition's title help direct the audience toward thinking about utopia, and maybe dystopia?

SY: I think the title helps narrow down the really broad idea of utopia to a smaller and more manageable set of operatives, that is, the "selling" of it, and how or whether it's bought. The exhibition's three music videos I call the Utopia Trilogy because they deal with the promotion and propagation of utopian dreams and visions. In *The highway is like a lion's mouth* (2018), there's the idea of the road to progress and regional integration; in *Da*

Da Company (2019), the idea of a return to the grandeur of past eras, with Won Alexander Cumyow—the first person of Chinese descent born in Canada and a proponent of the reform movement under the late Qing dynasty—as the promoter, or dreamer, of these visions; in *Houses of Tomorrow* (2019), the idea of cookie-cutter models of ideal homes for the next century. I am interested in the transmission of such visions, how they mutate in crossing cultural and national boundaries, and also in drawing analogies between the slogans of a national ethos at the 1933 world's fair in Chicago and what's going on in China today—the "Chinese Dream" versus the "American Dream," the "Century of Progress" versus the "Century of Humiliation." The 1933 fair was the rare case where the audience was able to see and experience in person the specifics of various visions for the future—the walking, dancing, and romancing dream Bing Crosby famously sang about that year in "Did You Ever See a Dream Walking?"

SK-C: There's a lot going on in these new works for *Silver moon or golden star*—references to songs and world's fairs, and domestic architecture—all conveyed through a proliferation of media. This kind of approach is characteristic of a generation of artists who, like you, trained as composers or performers in conservatories, and who have gone on to embrace diverse media, traditions, and gestures from outside the history of music composition. Some of them—Jennifer Walshe, Jessie Marino, Carolyn Chen, Neo Hülcker, James Saunders, Matthew Shlomowitz, and Steven Kazuo Takasugi, for example—have adopted the term "The New Discipline" to describe this turn in compositional practice.

SY: I was familiar with the work of some of these folks, but you drew my attention to Walshe's manifesto.[1] When John Cage started interning at architecture firms, Arnold Schoenberg became concerned that he was leaving music behind. So Cage wrote to assure Schoenberg that in making drawings he was still "faithful to music." I do think there is something very specific about a composer's training—it gives you a way of understanding and misreading the world that is quite unique, and also very hard to get rid of. While it is clear that the label "composer" is inadequate in describing the range of stuff I make, I think it's still useful for people to know my training. It might help them to understand why, for instance, I am obsessed with form, an obsession that sometimes expresses itself visually and spatially instead of sonically.

SK-C: I must admit that I wasn't sure if I was barking up the wrong tree there. And I guess on some level I was, but nevertheless I'd like to follow up on your response, starting with Cage's reassurance to Schoenberg that he'd be "faithful to music," and then the thought that it might be useful for your audience to know that you trained as a composer. The Cage story—as received not by Schoenberg but by the rest of us (who knows what Schoenberg thought?)—is often taken to be a declaration of Cage's deep commitment to music. But it could just as easily be understood as a bit of misdirection, like the magician who waves his left hand in the air as he retrieves the coin from his pocket with his right. Likewise, I wonder about how your audience should take not only the knowledge that you trained as a composer, but also the knowledge that you think it's "useful" for us to know that. Does this knowledge impose something upon our experience of the work that is not in the work? Is this information and its "usefulness" a kind of framing device that directs our attention away from what the work is actually doing, or not doing?

SY: Yes, labels and identifications of all kinds can distract an audience from what they might otherwise be focusing on—they can act as a smoke screen. I think artists use different languages to describe the things that they do, and the things they do might not ultimately be so different. For instance, I might think about how objects are placed in space as a kind of counterpoint to the different layers of sound occupying an exhibition's sonic space (headphones versus speakers in space versus radio broadcast). Here is a language of abstract concepts I'm familiar with, while artists with other backgrounds probably do the same thing but tell it differently. This is really different from saying, for example, that I'm trying to invent and innovate a kind of visual spatial equivalent of musical counterpoint—which I'm really not.

SK-C: Well, that leads me to ask about the factors, events, and opportunities that have encouraged you to pursue an "expanded" conception of composerly practice. Can you put your finger on certain turning points or catalysts?

SY: In the early 2000s, after my undergraduate studies in Australia, I came back to Hong Kong for a couple of years to work and start a master's degree. I was mostly writing concert music at that point. In Hong Kong I befriended the video artist Christopher Lau, who was working as the technical director at a new media art nonprofit called Videotage. I hung out there a bunch and went to their events, including a new media art festival called Microwave (which is still running). It opened up a whole other world to me. Chris and I met various media artists, including the poet Ron Lam, and the three of us worked together as a very loose collective. Chris and Ron were hugely influential for me. They had both gone to a school in Hong Kong that trained new media artists when this was really a newish thing. Many folks making new media art then came from backgrounds relevant to the work but not necessarily art related (computer science, engineering, biology, chemistry even). I was inspired by how Ron and Chris were always learning new codes and software—because the landscape of available tools out there changes so quickly. They'd dive right in and start making as soon as they'd gotten a hang of the basics. Their whole relationship to the idea of an artistic canon was fluid and inclusive. There are still some factions of the new media art community that are highly focused on the innovation of tools and more traditional ideas of craft, but then equally valid are folks who are hacking and messing about—just generally having fun with these tools.

Anyway, Ron, Chris, and I worked together for a while, and then I left for graduate school in the United States. By that point I had already made a few installation pieces with Chris, and I'd started toying with making video backdrops on my own, for my compositions. Later on, Chris and I won the Bloomberg Emerging Artist Award (in 2007), which gave us a grant to make an exhibition in a space with five rooms. We divided the rooms up between us and each made some installations. The show was all about hacked Nintendo Game Boys (fig. 2), and Chris and I learned a bunch about coding just for the exhibition. After that I got asked to make more work for gallery spaces—it started this whole parallel career to what I was doing in concert music.

fig. 2
Gameboy Haiku, 2007. Repurposed Nintendo Gameboy consoles, custom software

SK-C: As your practice continues to evolve, do you think you are part of a transition happening more broadly in art and music? Have you given any thought to why music is arriving at its "expanded" situation fifty years after the invocation of "expanded cinema," and forty years after Rosalind Krauss identified the "expanded field of sculpture"?

SY: The music world is still catching up to transitions that were already well underway in the larger art world when I started to get involved. Sound-installation-type pieces are kind of a staple now, even at places like Darmstadt, where I made a multichannel video and sound piece for the Internationale Ferienkurse für Neue Musik in 2016 (fig. 3), but that certainly wasn't the case when I first went there as a student a decade ago. I mean, they had only just started to regularly have non-European and women faculty members.

fig. 3
Installation view of Internationale Ferienkurse für Neue Musik, Darmstadt, Germany, 2016, with *historage*, *Notational Tendencies and Performance Processes*, 2016, three-channel video installation, ink and colored pencil on paper, repurposed rehearsal scores, archival materials

As to your question about the expanded situation of music, it's hard to say anything definitively. But at least pragmatically speaking, the delay might have something to do with various logistical aspects of technology and time-based media. Institutions got better at handling and archiving video art, media art, and the performing arts before sound art arrived on the scene. Most major museums now have an audiovisual specialist and a media art archivist to deal with things like the Max patch for a multichannel piece, and preparators now know to insulate the walls and put carpet down in a room when installing a piece with an important sound component. It is no longer acceptable for curators to just loop playlists on a speaker and call that a sound art presentation.

I think music has already broadened maybe everywhere *but* the academic institutions of music. Composition education is lagging behind especially, with composers inadequately prepared to deal with the much larger world of music outside of concert spaces. Some thinkers and practitioners in sound and music—I would say the most interesting ones—are working in departments of art, philosophy, media and communication studies, cultural studies, and performance studies. Meanwhile music departments—of course, some are better than others, but speaking generally—are still staffing faculties to teach the more traditional aspects of music. Music today is too big a field for the average-size university music department.

SK-C: Thinking back to what you said earlier about form—how it is kind of the bread and butter of composers—I want to ask you a question that has do with the relation of parts to a whole. It seems to me that the expansion, or "explosion" might be a better word, of your practice into such a dispersal of media forces the spectator to do something akin to forensic work in order to assemble a sense of what the work is and means. This explosion does some violence to the notion of form as a composer might conceive of it. I'm wondering how you understand the form of your work, and how you identify a unit of work? For example, are you conceiving of the exhibition *Silver moon or golden star* as comprised of many works? Or is the exhibition—the three animated music videos, the video of the performance, all the other materials—one big work?

SY: I think about form in a whole bunch of ways. Some forms are just sort of the back end of my process in putting things together, others have to do with how I structure the sensorial experience of walking through a space. Each of the four videos in this exhibition is an independent work that looks at the idea of utopia from different angles. Broadly speaking, you can think of the four rooms at the Smart Museum as three movements and a refrain. There is a kind of rhythm to how you experience the full space: the first room you enter is the smallest, the screen in the third room is double the size of the one in the first, and then we are back to a more intimate experience of film in the fourth room; the first and second rooms are blasting music at you via stereo PA systems, the third room climaxes with a multichannel eight-speaker setup, and finally, the fourth returns you to a more intimate experience, with headphones. Another thing is, because the Smart Museum has really high ceilings, I am dropping the ceiling of the second room significantly—when you emerge from it into the next room the sights and sounds of the exhibition space will sort of peak. And then there are the music and visual elements of the videos themselves. *The highway* and *Da Da Company* are similar in that they both have a weird binary form that takes a sharp turn in the middle. *Houses of Tomorrow* is the most fragmented musically. Visually, in the music videos, there's another thing going on: the jumps between the animated and filmed footage increase in frequency, so that *Houses of Tomorrow*, in the third room, is basically half animation and half filmed footage. In the fourth room, *The world falls apart* is mostly filmed filmed documentation of a performance.

SK-C: W. B. Yeats once said "a poem comes right with a click like a closing box." But in your individual projects and exhibitions, the click is often missing. In other words, the meaning of the work is often left unclicked, or unresolved (to think of it musically). There's a tension between coherence and incoherence. I'm often left feeling that I've been provided with some orientation, but also disorientation. How conscious is this denial of closure on your part? And what do you think is achieved by this openness or ambiguity?

SY: I am aware of it in the sense that I know I am a messy thinker. It takes time for me to make up my mind, and all the confusion and incoherence is in the work. It's never a strategy to achieve a specific kind of disorientation in the audience or something like that. If anything, there's always a battle I'll realize I've given up fighting. To keep thinking about whether something is too obvious or too obscure paralyzes me. It takes all the fun out of the making.

SK-C: It's pretty clear that, formally speaking, you're not a minimalist. In fact, your work lands more in the neighborhood of the Wagnerian *Gesamtkunstwerk*, or total work of art. This, of course, would be a production that involves music, movement, image, text, and sets. Additionally, in your work there is animation, appropriated media, objects, drawings, documents, and more.

As many critics have observed, the totalizing impulse of the *Gesamtkunstwerk* sits in uncomfortable relation with Richard Wagner's politics and with the totalitarianism of the Nazis, who considered him a heroic precursor. But thinking about this in the midst of our contemporary predicament, the *Gesamtkunstwerk* might parallel capitalism's total consumption of the earth's resources. Your video *Da Da Company* is at least partly concerned with this—with consumerism, with capitalism's manufacture of desire, with floods and environmental catastrophe—and not so much utopia as dystopia. Can you say something about the overloaded aspects of your work in general, or of this exhibition in particular? And can you relate the overload of the *Gesamtkunstwerk* to the themes and meanings of your work? I guess this is a question about how form relates to content.

SY: Let me break your line of inquiry down into several parts. About the sheer amount of stuff that's going on in the work, I think you're referring to the presentation of some of my *Muted Situations* (2014–ongoing) (fig. 4), which can end up being pretty basic. Much of what I made before *Nocturne* (2015) and *Canon* (2016) was also pretty "clean" and focused conceptually.

fig. 4
Installation view of *SUPERPOSITION: Equilibrium & Engagement*, Twenty-First Biennale
of Sydney, 2018, with *Muted Situations #22: Muted Tchaikovsky's 5th*, 2018

So it really does depend on the specific work, but it's true that
my recent shows, since *Songs for Disaster Relief* (Hong Kong
Pavilion, Fifty-Seventh Venice Biennale, 2017), have tended to be
pretty full of stuff, with saturated colors and lots of objects and
multichannel sound. That's just where my mind is at right now.
Part of it is how my brain processes information. If you look at the
images in a piece like *Da Da Company*, it's a sprawling network
of histories and references. I used to worry about too much
information and what it does to an audience, but I have made
peace with that now. People will make their own connections
between bits and pieces to generate a reading, and as long as
the form of the thing keeps it all together, space is made for the
"processing" to happen.

With animation, which is still relatively new to me, I feel like its
production workflow just sets my maximalist self free. There isn't

as much of a delay (compared to shooting video) between when an image comes to me and when the image can be made in the computer. About the issue of control, I am the first to admit that I'm a bit of a control freak. As a student I did start out writing a kind of aleatoric music, with super short gestures, but I was not happy with how much control I had to relinquish—even with a lot of detail in the notation, which doesn't really guarantee translation into performance. This is at least partly how I've ended up writing electroacoustic music almost exclusively these days. In the more extreme of these compositions, there is a linear electronic track that behaves sort of like an audible metronome to keep the musicians in time. I once wrote a piece for the Mivos Quartet called *17* (2013), which has the electronic part doubling the players in parallel motion, and at a pretty insane tempo. You can really hear it when the players are out of sync—the poor souls of Mivos practiced really hard to have this never happen in performance. Art is where you can safely experiment and have fun playing with ideas and relationships, though. Preferences and habits of working probably say more about the creator's neurosis and trauma than politics. Sometimes I think of the very specific kind of daze that video games manage to induce in players— the total takeover of their senses and mental-processing power, which is at once total engagement and detachment—as being very symptomatic of our times. This is not to say I think it's a good thing.

I am still not answering you, though, about how form relates to content in this exhibition. The short answer is that it's a bit early, I am still composing the music for two of the videos. I also want to point out—though I know this is not what you meant—that I am not wedded to the idea that form and content have to relate in the sense that they inform or clarify each other. Form can be the architecture that provides space for mental play, or it can be a certain sequence of affective qualities that sort of makes sense on its own, or it can contradict the content.

SK-C: That is a really nice description of your feelings about form. But it kind of dodges the content side. To get at that, I want to follow up on your comment in an interview for your exhibition *It's a heaven over there* (2019) at Centre A in Vancouver. There you explain to Godfre Leung how the videos you're showing at the Smart Museum relate to each other and to the 1933 world's fair in Chicago. You say:

> The 1933 World's Fair carried the subtitle "A Century of Progress." It was an interesting time for an event like that. The Great Depression was well underway, and shit was about to hit the fan with the Second World War. It was also an era when all the different ideologies, from fascism to communism to capitalism, were still very much in play. Compare that with now, when nothing is in play anymore. We have truly reached the end of history, not in the sense that Francis Fukuyama had defined it, where capitalism is the endgame, but with a failure of the imagination to envision a future that is better than now.[2]

I have to ask, if we are indeed at the end of history, where imagination has arrived at a terminal failure to envision a better future, what is the relation of your recent works—or maybe just *Silver moon or golden star*—to this situation? Do these videos merely report the news that we're fucked? Do they attempt to wake us from our imaginative coma? Are they a palliative, holding our hand through the end times? Or something else? The big question is: What is the role of art at the end of history?

SY: Making work, for me, is trying to figure things out. I'm not evading your question about content or refusing to state a position, but I can't do any of the things you listed because I haven't yet made up my mind about the questions I'm dealing with, and I'm not in a rush to do so—which is okay because I'm not trying to change anybody's mind. Art deals with truth and truth is complicated. This is particularly important given the sort of time we're in now. Art continues to be a place where the complexity of truth is not sanitized, where truth stays messy, self-contradictory, uncomfortable, and complicated.

NOTES

1   Jennifer Walshe, "The New Discipline," Borealis Festival website, January 2016, http://www. borealisfestival.no/2016/the-new-discipline-4/.

2   "Places That Are Not A Place: Samson Young in conversation with Godfre Leung," in *Samson Young: It's a heaven over there*, ed. Godfre Leung (Vancouver: Centre A, 2019), 7.

SUMMER PALACE ROAD.
PEIPING TO WESTERN HILLS
STONE ABOUT 1708 A.D.
CHINA

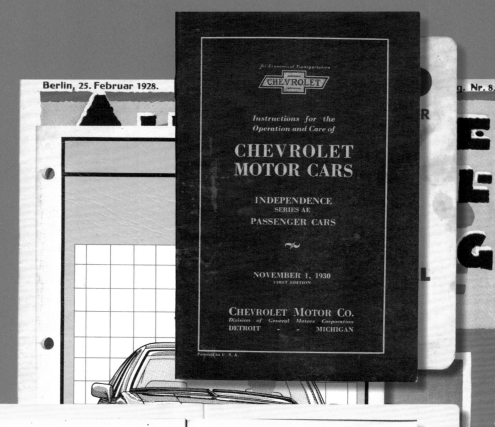

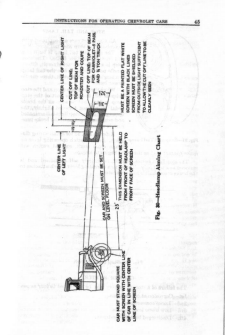

Cover and interior pages of the booklet *Instructions for the Operation and Care of Chevrolet Motor Cars*, published by Chevrolet Motor Company, 1930. Research material for *The highway is like a lion's mouth*, 2018

Left fragment (partial page 18)

18

Sp...
met...

A...
idea...
Ford...
Any...
car...
whe...

C...
the s...
whe...
raise...
the...
finge...

ANALYSIS OF GEA...

Gear Howl and Whi...

When disassembling the...
gear noise, it is assumed...
items and station wago...
checked as possible caus...

The noises described un...
specific causes that can b...
the unit is disassemble...
course, the type of noise...
driving conditions.

Chuckle

Chuckle that occurs on th...
ally caused by excessive...
gear wear; or by a damag...
the pinion or ring gear.

Any damage to a gear too...
noise identical to chuckle...
or ridge on the edge of a...
noise (Figure 41).

Figure 41 — Damaged Ge...

You can often correct this...
noise simply by cleaning up...
a small grinding wheel.

If either gear is scored or d...
must be replaced. Also, if t...
the carrier and housing m...
particles that could cause...
damaged parts in the axle...

Center top — Pages 48–49

A discharged battery will freeze at a little below the freezing point.
A fully charged battery will not freeze, even at temperatures as low as 30° below zero; therefore, keep the battery fully charged.

GENERAL LUBRICATION

Your Chevrolet dealer is equipped to render complete lubrication service. We recommend that you take advantage of his specialized equipment and trained men when in need of this type of service.

The chart on lubrication (Fig. 34) shows where and when to lubricate different units of a Chevrolet car. Oil and grease are much cheaper than repair bills and should be applied regularly, if you are to secure a maximum of useful service from your car.

To assist in meeting this problem on lubrication, the Chevrolet Motor Company has the following recommendations to make, with respect to oils:

We do not recommend the use of so-called re-refined oils, as we find that unless extreme care is used in the refining process, they are wholly unsuitable for use in Chevrolet cars.

For proper Motor Lubrication, a high grade, well refined oil is essential.

For the First 500 Miles—
Under no circumstances should an oil having a body heavier than that of SAE viscosity No. 20 and with a zero pour test be used in motors of new cars.

For Summer Use—
After the first 500 Miles an oil having a body of SAE viscosity No. 20 may be used.

After the first 2,000 Miles an oil having a body of SAE viscosity No. 30 may be used in motors which are subject to prolonged high speed driving.

For Winter Use—
An oil having a body of SAE viscosity No. 20 and with a zero pour test is recommended. Such an oil should be satisfactory down to temperatures of from 10° to 15° above zero Fahrenheit, below which temperatures an oil of SAE viscosity No. 10 and with a zero or sub-zero pour test should be used. If such an oil is not procurable, an oil of SAE viscosity No. 20 diluted with 10% kerosene, would give equal satisfaction.

LUBRICATION OF BRAKE LINKAGE

In addition to the various grease connections that are lubricated every 500 miles, the brake linkage, or clevis pins, rods and etc., should be lubricated with a good grade of machine oil which will insure the correct operation of these units.

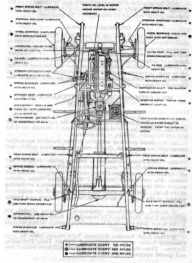

LUBRICATE EVERY 500 MILES
LUBRICATE EVERY 1000 MILES
LUBRICATE EVERY 2000 MILES

Fig. 34—Lubrication Chart

Right fragment

...repeat steps 1-4 on the

...allowable up to 0.635
...reduced to 0.127 mm
...C-washer that holds
...le gear (Figure 44).

SHIM —
INSTALL BEHIND
C-WASHER

SHIM
STOCK

E3758-1A

...Play Correction

To reduce the clearance, cut a shim in the pattern of the washer and install it behind the washer. Do not reduce the end play to less than 0.127 mm (0.005 inch).

...n the driveline, but not
...mine whether driveline
...ke a check of the total

...e companion flange and
...o that the flange cannot

...keep it from turning.

...until you "feel" it in a
...k marker on the side of
...e center of the wheel

Center — mid fragments

(1/8 inch), it is advisable to replace the gear set.

Knock

20

Bottom center — Pages 20–21

If, at any time, the clutch pedal is more than ⅓" away from the end of the slot in the floor board, when the clutch is fully engaged, the clutch pedal adjusting bolt should be turned to the left until the proper clearance is obtained.

CARE OF CLUTCH

Do not lubricate the clutch.

The clutch is designed so that the clutch throwout collar and pilot bearing are both self lubricating and no oil or grease need be applied at these points; also care should be exercised to keep oil and grease away from the clutch disc and clutch facings.

It is well, with the first indication of any difficulty with the clutch, to consult the nearest Chevrolet Dealer or Service Station.

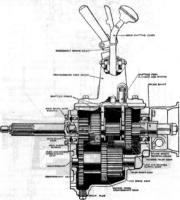

Fig. 9—Transmission

Do not disengage the clutch when starting the motor.
Do not ride the clutch pedal.
Do not attempt to hold the car on a hill or grade by slipping the clutch. This will wear the clutch facings and throwout bearing.

TRANSMISSION

The transmission is of the selective type, having three speeds forward and one reverse.

The fundamental requirement is to first engage the gears so that the entire tooth "face" of the sliding gears mesh with those on the countershaft and, second, to properly lubricate all working parts. Proper engagement can be had by being sure, when shifting gears, that the gear shift lever travels as far forward, or backward, as it will go, before re-engaging the clutch.

LUBRICATION OF TRANSMISSION

To lubricate the transmission, fill every 1,000 miles with a heavy oil such as 600W, not grease, so that the oil level stands even with the opening in the filler boss on the right side of the case. In cold weather we recommend the addition of a pint of light engine oil to the heavy oil in the transmission, which improves the lubricating qualities and makes it easier to shift gears and start the motor.

Once every 2,000 miles it is a good plan to wash out the transmission with a light oil, to remove any chips of metal knocked off the gears, or other foreign substances, such as grit or dirt. To do this, remove the drain plug at the bottom of the transmission case and allow the oil to drain off, after which flush out the case thoroughly and refill with a heavy oil, such as specified in Fig. 34.

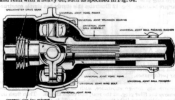

Fig. 10—Universal Joint

Cover and interior pages of the booklet *Ford Passenger Car Owner's Manual*,
published by Ford Motor Company, 1950. Research material for *The highway is like
a lion's mouth*, 2018

Berlin, 25. Februar 1928.

g. Nr. 8.

1950 **FORD**

PASSENGER CAR

FORD

OWNER'S MANUAL

FORD MOTOR CO.
FORD DIVISION

Getting Acquainted

Before you actual-
ly drive your new car,
you will want first to
become familiar with
the controls and in-
struments that you
use. Controls are
grouped for conven-
ience, yet are easy to
see and read.

The instruments
are located directly in
front of the driver.
The fuel gauge, oil
pressure gauge, engine temperature gauge, and the
ammeter are grouped around the speedometer. The
entire group is recessed behind a single, non-glaring
dial glass for easy reading. The numerals and point-
ers on all instruments glow at night; they are illumi-
nated by "black light" when the lights of the car are
turned on.

Form the habit of frequently glancing at the instruments as you drive. They let you know how the engine
and other important units are working. With the ex-
ception of the speedometer all of the instruments
are electric. The instrument marked OIL shows the
oil pressure to the engine bearings. The gauge marked

1

further comments are necessary.

056

Page 18

Spots on the upholstery can be removed by the same methods as used in cleaning quality furniture.

After removing a spot of any kind, it may be a good idea to go over the entire seat using Ford foam type upholstery cleaner. Any metal trim on the inside of the car can be wiped with a damp cloth when it becomes dusty or dirty.

Changing tires—The jack is of the safety type that cannot be tripped when it is supporting the car. To raise the car, position the jack under the bumper properly, put the control finger so that it points upward, and operate the jack using the wheel nut wrench as a handle. Pry off the hub cap to gain access to the wheel nuts.

It is recommended that the tires be cross-switched twice a year or every 5000 miles. The tires should be cross-switched as shown.

See that the tires on your car are properly inflated at all times. Correct air pressures are listed below:

Tire Size	Front	Rear
6:70 x 15	24 lbs.	21 lbs.
6:00 x 16	28 lbs.	25 lbs.
7:10 x 15	25 lbs.	30 lbs.

Lubrication and Maintenance

A car as well as any piece of precision machinery requires lubrication. It is necessary to keep a film of oil or grease between moving parts, in order to lengthen their life. See to it that your car is properly lubricated at all times.

All the lubrication recommendations are listed here. Your Ford dealer is best qualified and equipped to perform these services for you.

Table of Capacities	6-Cyl.	8-Cyl.
Engine Oil	4 qt.	4 qt.
Extra for Filter Change	1 qt.	1 qt.
Transmission	3¼ pt.	3¼ pt.
With Overdrive	4½ pt.	4½ pt.
Axle	3½ pt.	3½ pt.
Gasoline Tank	16 gal.	16 gal.
Station Wagon	19 gal.	19 gal.
Water (Heater—1 qt. extra)	16 qt.	21 qt.

The engine oil should be changed four times a year (every 2,000 miles). If the weather that you expect will be Summer weather (above freezing) use S.A.E. 20 or 20 W. In Winter weather (below freezing) use 10 W. For extreme cold (colder than 10° below

19

Page 20

zero) use 10 W diluted with 1 pint of kerosene. Have the oil checked regularly. The capacity for either the 6-cylinder or the 8-cylinder engine is 4 quarts, except when the filter cartridge is changed, then use an extra quart.

Pressure gun fittings—Units equipped with pressure gun fittings can be lubricated only with a pressure type grease gun. Force grease into each fitting every 1000 miles. Fittings that become plugged (frozen) should be replaced at time of lubrication. These fittings are located as follows:

Upper suspension arms—three fittings each side of car. Reach the inside rear fitting from under the hood.

King pins—two fittings each side of car.

Lower suspension arms—three fittings each side.

Tie rods—four fittings, one at each end of both tie rods.

Intermediate link—one fitting at each end of link.

Steering idler arm—one fitting at top end.

Clutch and brake pedals—one fitting at each arm.

Penetrating oil—The following listed items should be sprayed with dripless penetrating oil at the time of an oil change:

Clutch equalizer-to-yoke rod.

Clutch release equalizer felt washer.

Gearshift rod end and clutch release rod.

Several units on the vehicle do not need lubrication. However, they require service at regular intervals.

Page 21

The oil filter cartridge should be changed at least at time of every oil change, or whenever the dipstick shows dirty oil (approximately 4000 to 5000 miles).

The engine oil filler cap serves as the intake screen for the engine ventilating system. If this becomes plugged, oil loss will result. Occasionally clean the screen and saturate it with engine oil.

Oil bath air cleaner—Remove the cover and inspect the oil at time of oil change. Clean and then refill the sump to the full level mark with engine oil. The air cleaner should be serviced more frequently under severe dust conditions.

Dry type air cleaner—Wash the filter pack in solvent. Allow it to dry and dip it in engine oil.

Door latches, hood latch, and rear deck lid latch should be lubricated with stainless stick lubricant at time of oil change.

Door hinges, outside door handles, and deck lid hinges—Apply dripless penetrating oil at time of oil change.

Cover and interior pages of the booklet *Car and Light Truck Diagnosis and Repair:
Noise, Vibration, Harshness*, published by Ford Motor Company, 1984. Research
material for *The highway is like a lion's mouth*, 2018

CAR AND LIGHT TRUCK
DIAGNOSIS AND REPAIR

NOISE
VIBRATION
HARSHNESS

Ford Parts and Service Division
Training and Publications Department

Berlin, 25. Februar 1928.   29. Jahrgang. Nr. 8.

Blick von der Bergstraße zum Monte Bré auf den Monte San Salvatore bei Lugano.

VERLAG V. KLASING & Cº G·M·B·H BERLIN W9·LINKSTR·38

DRIVE AXLE

ANALYSIS OF GEAR NOISE

Gear Howl and Whine

When disassembling the axle to diagnose and correct gear noise, it is assumed that the tires, exhaust, trim items and station wagon roof racks have first been checked as possible causes.

The noises described under "Road Test" usually have specific causes that can be diagnosed by observation as the unit is disassembled. The initial clues are, of course, the type of noise heard on the road test and the driving conditions.

Chuckle

Chuckle that occurs on the coast driving phase is usually caused by excessive clearance due to differential gear wear; or by a damaged tooth on the coast side of the pinion or ring gear.

Any damage to a gear tooth on the coast side can cause a noise identical to chuckle. Even a very small tooth nick or ridge on the edge of a tooth is enough to cause the noise (Figure 41).

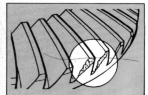

Figure 41 — Damaged Gear Tooth

You can often correct this condition and remove the noise simply by cleaning up the tooth nick or ridge with a small grinding wheel.

If either gear is scored or damaged badly, the gear set must be replaced. Also, if there is metal broken loose, the carrier and housing must be cleaned to remove particles that could cause damage later. Any other damaged parts in the axle must be replaced.

To check the gear set, remove as much lubricant as possible from the gears with clean solvent. Wipe the gears dry or blow them dry with compressed air. Look for scored or damaged teeth (Figures 41 and 42). Also look for cracks or other damage.

Figure 42 — Scored Gear Set

If the cleaned up or damaged area is larger than 3.2 mm (1/8 inch), it is advisable to replace the gear set.

Knock

Knock, which can occur on all driving phases, has several causes. In most cases, you will discover one of the following conditions.

1. A gear tooth damaged on the drive side is a common cause of the knock. This can usually be corrected by grinding the damaged area.

2. Occasionally, the ring gear bolts will knock against the inside of the carrier casting. The cause may be too little clearance, due to casting flash or bumps. In this case, the carrier can be removed and interference points ground out.

Another possibility is simply that one or more bolts are slightly backed out. Proper tightening will correct the condition.

40

DRIVE AXLE

3. Knock is also characteristic of excessive end play in the axle shafts. Up to 0.254 mm (0.010 inch) is allowed in most axles. However, it may be as high as 1.14 mm (0.045 inch); so that knock occurs even in design conditions. The frequency of knock will be less because the axle shaft speed is slower than the driveshaft.

NOTE: BE SURE TO MEASURE THE END PLAY WITH A DIAL INDICATOR; NOT BY FEEL. A "GUESSTIMATE" USUALLY FEELS LIKE FAR MORE END PLAY THAN THERE ACTUALLY IS.

AXLE SHAFT END PLAY CHECK (INTEGRAL AXLE)

1. Remove wheel and tire, brake drum or rotor.

2. Mount a dial indicator on the brake backing plate or caliper frame, and place the indicator stem on the axle shaft flange (Figure 43).

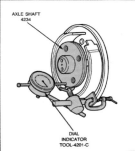

Figure 43 — Measuring Axle Shaft End Play

3. Push the shaft inward until it bottoms and zero the dial indicator.

4. Pull the axle outward until it bottoms again and read the total end play.

5. Remove the dial indicator and repeat steps 1-4 on the opposite side.

On the integral axle, end play is allowable up to 0.635 mm (0.025 inch), but can be reduced to 0.127 mm (0.005 inch). It is controlled by the C-washer that holds the shaft in the pocket of the side gear (Figure 44).

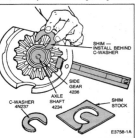

Figure 44 — Integral Axle End Play Correction

To reduce the clearance, cut a shim in the pattern of the washer and install it behind the washer. Do not reduce the end play to less than 0.127 mm (0.005 inch).

Clunk

Clunk is due to backlash in the driveline, but not necessarily in the axle. To determine whether driveline clunk is caused by the axle, make a check of the total axle backlash as follows:

1. Raise the vehicle on a frame or twin post hoist so that the rear wheels are free.

2. Clamp a bar between the axle companion flange and a part of the frame or body so that the flange cannot move.

3. Lock the left rear wheel to keep it from turning.

4. Turn the right wheel slowly until you "feel" it in a drive condition. Hold a chalk marker on the side of the tire 12 inches from the center of the wheel (Figure 45).

41

059

Berlin, 25. Februar 1928.   29. Jahrgang. Nr. 8.

ALLGEMEINE AVTOMOBIL-ZEITVNG

Blick von der Bergstraße zum Monte Bré auf den Monte San Salvatore bei Lugano.

VERLAG V·KLASING & C.º G·M·B·H BERLIN W9·LINKSTR·38

44

The ligh
ground retu
light (and do
The ligh
instrument p

Fig. 28

The ope
pressible be
means of a t
on the toe b
the clutch
Fig. 28 l
lamp with t
bulb, as well
and special
The spec
is made up c
which effect
beams of li
desired light pattern. This iens
is used in connection with a plain
reflector.
Proper headlamp adjustment may be obtained by following the
instructions outlined in Fig. 30. The chart is self-explanatory and no
further comments are necessary.

Fig. 29—Headlamp Lens

CAR MUST STAND
WITH SCREEN
OF CAR IN LINE
LINE OF SCREEN

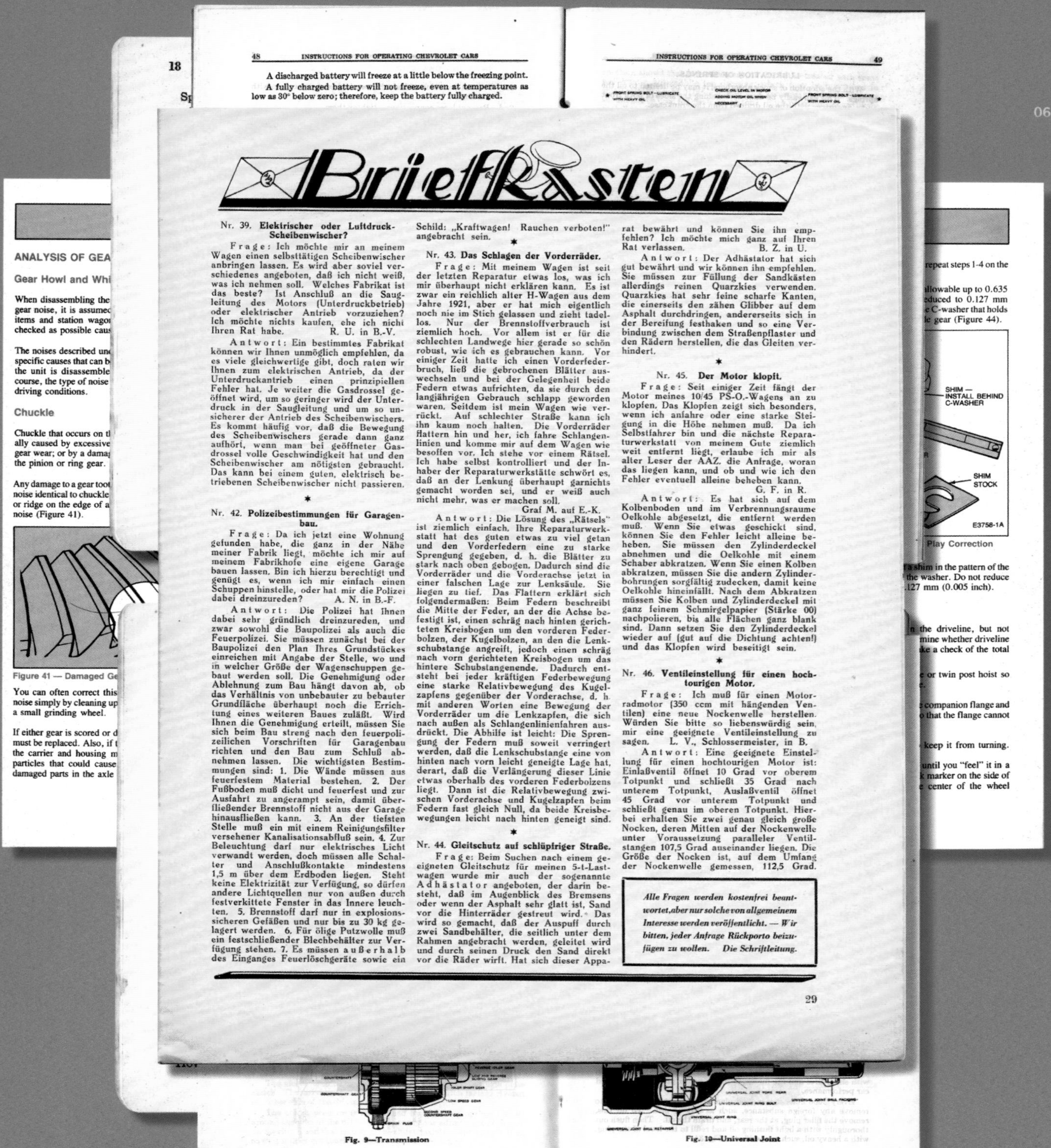

A discharged battery will freeze at a little below the freezing point.
A fully charged battery will not freeze, even at temperatures as low as 30° below zero; therefore, keep the battery fully charged.

ANALYSIS OF GEA[R]

Gear Howl and Whi[ne]

When disassembling the … gear noise, it is assume[d] … items and station wago[n] … checked as possible caus[e]

The noises described un[der] … specific causes that can b[e] … the unit is disassemble[d] … course, the type of noise … driving conditions.

Chuckle

Chuckle that occurs on t[he] … ally caused by excessive … gear wear; or by a damag[ed] … the pinion or ring gear.

Any damage to a gear too[th] … noise identical to chuckle … or ridge on the edge of a … noise (Figure 41).

Figure 41 — Damaged Ge[ar]

You can often correct this … noise simply by cleaning up … a small grinding wheel.

If either gear is scored or d[amaged] … must be replaced. Also, if t[he] … the carrier and housing m[ust] … particles that could cause … damaged parts in the axle …

Briefkasten

Nr. 39. Elektrischer oder Luftdruck-Scheibenwischer?

Frage: Ich möchte mir an meinem Wagen einen selbsttätigen Scheibenwischer anbringen lassen. Es wird aber soviel verschiedenes angeboten, daß ich nicht weiß, was ich nehmen soll. Welches Fabrikat ist das beste? Ist Anschluß an die Saugleitung des Motors (Unterdruckbetrieb) oder elektrischer Antrieb vorzuziehen? Ich möchte nichts kaufen, ehe ich nicht Ihren Rat habe. R. U. in B.-V.

Antwort: Ein bestimmtes Fabrikat können wir Ihnen unmöglich empfehlen, da es viele gleichwertige gibt, doch raten wir Ihnen zum elektrischen Antrieb, da der Unterdruckantrieb einen prinzipiellen Fehler hat. Je weiter die Gasdrossel geöffnet wird, um so geringer wird der Unterdruck in der Saugleitung und um so unsicherer der Antrieb des Scheibenwischers. Es kommt häufig vor, daß die Bewegung des Scheibenwischers gerade dann ganz aufhört, wenn man bei geöffneter Gasdrossel volle Geschwindigkeit braucht und der Scheibenwischer am nötigsten gebraucht. Das kann bei einem guten, elektrisch betriebenen Scheibenwischer nicht passieren.

Nr. 42. Polizeibestimmungen für Garagenbau.

Frage: Da ich jetzt eine Wohnung gefunden habe, die ganz in der Nähe meiner Fabrik liegt, möchte ich mir auf meinem Fabrikhofe eine eigene Garage bauen lassen. Bin ich hierzu berechtigt und genügt es, wenn ich mir einfach einen Schuppen hinstelle, oder hat mir der Polizei dabei dreinzureden? A. N. in B.-F.

Antwort: Die Polizei hat Ihnen dabei sehr gründlich dreinzureden, und zwar sowohl die Baupolizei als auch die Feuerpolizei. Sie müssen zunächst bei der Baupolizei den Plan Ihres Grundstückes einreichen mit Angabe der Stelle, wo und in welcher Größe der Wagenschuppen gebaut werden soll. Die Genehmigung oder Ablehnung zum Bau hängt davon ab, ob das Niveau von unbebauter oder bebauter Grundfläche überhaupt noch die Errichtung eines weiteren Baues zuläßt. Wird Ihnen die Genehmigung erteilt, müssen Sie sich beim Bau streng nach den feuerpolizeilichen Vorschriften für Garagenbau richten und den Bau zum Schluß abnehmen lassen. Die wichtigsten Bestimmungen sind: 1. Die Wände müssen aus feuerfestem Material bestehen. 2. Der Fußboden muß dicht und feuerfest und zur Ausfahrt so angeramt sein, damit abfließender Brennstoff nicht aus der Garage hinausfließen kann. 3. An der tiefsten Stelle muß ein mit einem Reinigungsfilter versehener Kanalisationsabfluß sein. 4. Zur Beleuchtung darf nur elektrisches Licht verwandt werden, doch müssen alle Schalter und Anschlußkontakte mindestens 1,5 m über dem Erdboden liegen. Steht keine Elektrizität zur Verfügung, so dürfen andere Lichtquellen nur von außen durch festverkittete Fenster das Innere leuchten. 5. Brennstoff darf nur in explosionssicheren Gefäßen und nur bis zu 30 kg gelagert werden. 6. Für ölige Putzwolle muß ein festschließender Blechbehälter zur Verfügung stehen. 7. Es müssen außerhalb des Einganges Feuerlöschgeräte sowie ein Schild: „Kraftwagen! Rauchen verboten!" angebracht sein.

Nr. 43. Das Schlagen der Vorderräder.

Frage: Mit meinem Wagen ist seit der letzten Reparatur etwas los, was ich mir überhaupt nicht erklären kann. Es ist zwar ein reichlich alter H-Wagen aus dem Jahre 1921, aber er hat mich eigentlich noch nie im Stich gelassen und reitet tadellos. Nur der Brennstoffverbrauch ist ziemlich hoch. Vor allem ist er für die schlechten Landwege hier gerade so schön robust, wie ich es gebrauchen kann. Vor einiger Zeit hatte ich einen Vorderfederbruch, ließ die gebrochenen Blätter auswechseln und bei der Gelegenheit beide Federn etwas aufrichten, da sie durch den langjährigen Gebrauch schlapp geworden waren. Seitdem ist mein Wagen wie verrückt. Auf schlechter Straße kann ich ihn kaum noch halten. Die Vorderräder flattern hin und her, ich fahre Schlangenlinien und komme mir aus dem Wagen wie besoffen vor. Ich stehe vor einem Rätsel. Ich habe selbst kontrolliert und der Inhaber der Reparaturwerkstätte schwört es, daß an der Lenkung überhaupt garnichts gemacht worden sei, und er weiß auch nicht mehr, was er machen soll. Graf M. auf E.-K.

Antwort: Die Lösung des „Rätsels" ist ziemlich einfach. Ihre Reparaturwerkstatt hat des guten etwas zu viel getan und den Vorderfedern eine zu starke Sprengung gegeben, d. h. die Blätter zu stark nach oben gebogen. Dadurch sind die Vorderräder und die Vorderachse jetzt in einer falschen Lage zur Lenksäule. Das Flattern erklärt sich folgendermaßen: Beim Federn beschreibt die Mitte der Feder, an der die Achse befestigt ist, einen schräg nach hinten gerichteten Kreisbogen um den vorderen Federbolzen, an den die Lenkschubstange angreift, jedoch einen schräg nach vorn gerichteten Kreisbogen um das hintere Schubstangenende. Dadurch entsteht bei jeder kräftigen Federbewegung eine starke Relativbewegung des Kugelzapfens gegenüber der Vorderachse, d. h. mit anderen Worten eine Bewegung der Vorderräder um die Lenkzapfen, die sich nach außen als Schlangenlinienfahren ausdrückt. Die Abhilfe ist leicht: Die Sprengung der Federn muß soweit verringert werden, daß die Lenkschubstange eine von hinten nach vorn leicht geneigte Lage hat, derart, daß die Verlängerung dieser Linie etwas oberhalb des vorderen Federbolzens liegt. Dann ist die Relativbewegung zwischen Vorderachse und Kugelzapfen der Federn fast gleich Null, da beide Kreisbewegungen leicht nach hinten geneigt sind.

Nr. 44. Gleitschutz auf schlüpfriger Straße.

Frage: Beim Suchen nach einem geeigneten Gleitschutz für meinen 5-t-Lastwagen wurde mir auch der sogenannte Adhästator angeboten, der darin besteht, daß im Augenblick des Bremsens oder wenn der Asphalt sehr glatt ist, Sand vor die Hinterräder gestreut wird. - Das wird so gemacht, daß der Auspuff durch zwei Sandbehälter, die seitlich unter dem Rahmen angebracht werden, geleitet wird und durch seinen Druck den Sand direkt vor die Räder wirft. Hat sich dieser Appa-rat bewährt und können Sie ihn empfehlen? Ich möchte mich ganz auf Ihren Rat verlassen. B. Z. in U.

Antwort: Der Adhästator hat sich gut bewährt und wir können ihn empfehlen. Sie müssen zur Füllung der Sandkästen allerdings reinen Quarzkies verwenden. Quarzkies hat sehr feine scharfe Kanten, die einerseits den zähen Glibber auf dem Asphalt durchdringen, andererseits sich in der Bereifung festhaken und so eine Verbindung zwischen dem Straßenpflaster und den Rädern herstellen, die das Gleiten verhindert.

Nr. 45. Der Motor klopft.

Frage: Seit einiger Zeit fängt der Motor meines 10/45 PS-O-Wagens an zu klopfen. Das Klopfen zeigt sich besonders, wenn ich anfahre oder eine starke Steigung in die Höhe nehmen muß. Da ich Selbstfahrer bin und die nächste Reparaturwerkstatt von meinem Gute ziemlich weit entfernt liegt, erlaube ich mir als alter Leser der AAZ, die Anfrage, woran das liegen kann, und ob und wie ich den Fehler eventuell alleine beheben kann. G. F. in R.

Antwort: Es hat sich auf dem Kolbenboden und im Verbrennungsraume Oelkohle abgesetzt, die entfernt werden muß. Wenn Sie etwas geschickt sind, können Sie den Fehler leicht alleine beheben. Sie müssen den Zylinderdeckel abnehmen und die Oelkohle mit einem Schaber abkratzen. Wenn Sie einen Kolben abkratzen, müssen Sie die andern Zylinderbohrungen sorgfältig zudecken, damit keine Oelkohle hineinfällt. Nach dem Abkratzen müssen Sie Kolben und Zylinderdeckel mit ganz feinem Schmirgelpapier (Stärke 00) nachpolieren, bis alle Flächen ganz blank sind. Dann setzen Sie den Zylinderdeckel wieder auf (gut auf die Dichtung achten!) und das Klopfen wird beseitigt sein.

Nr. 46. Ventileinstellung für einen hochtourigen Motor.

Frage: Ich muß für einen Motorradmotor (350 ccm mit hängenden Ventilen) eine neue Nockenwelle herstellen. Würden Sie bitte so liebenswürdig sein, mir eine geeignete Ventileinstellung zu sagen. L. V., Schlossermeister, in B.

Antwort: Eine geeignete Einstellung für einen hochtourigen Motor ist: Einlaßventil öffnet 10 Grad vor oberem Totpunkt und schließt 35 Grad nach unterem Totpunkt, Auslaßventil öffnet 45 Grad vor unterem Totpunkt und schließt genau im oberen Totpunkt. Hierbei erhalten Sie zwei genau gleiche große Nocken, deren Mitten auf der Nockenwelle unter Voraussetzung 107,5 Grad auseinander liegen. Die Größe der Nocken, auf dem Umfang der Nockenwelle gemessen, 112,5 Grad.

Alle Fragen werden kostenfrei beantwortet, aber nur solche von allgemeinem Interesse werden veröffentlicht. – Wir bitten, jeder Anfrage Rückporto beizufügen zu wollen. Die Schriftleitung.

repeat steps 1-4 on the …

allowable up to 0.635 … reduced to 0.127 mm … C-washer that holds … gear (Figure 44).

SHIM — INSTALL BEHIND C-WASHER

SHIM STOCK

E3758-1A

Play Correction

…a shim in the pattern of the … the washer. Do not reduce … 127 mm (0.005 inch).

…n the driveline, but no[t] … mine whether driveline … ke a check of the total …

… or twin post hoist so …

…e companion flange and … o that the flange cannot …

… keep it from turning … until you "feel" it in a … k marker on the side of … e center of the wheel

Fig. 9—Transmission

Fig. 10—Universal Joint

061

Stay in Touch

TUESDAY, APRIL 17, 1984

All you need to know about yesterday and today, plus a few surprises. Edited by David Dale

Travel tips

This item will explain how you can obtain $12,720 worth of first class return air travel to Europe for just $2,544, a feat achieved by Neville and Jill Wran last week. No, you don't have to be Premier of NSW. The answer is: become a Qantas employee, rise to a senior position, go on leave of absence, and then get retrenched. Mrs Wran used to work for Qantas, and as one of the airline's three international sales...

forests of South-East Asia. Offspring of the birds flown to Bangkok eventually will be released into Thailand's Huai Kha Kheeng Forest Sanctuary.

Going, going

Blame It On Rio, Michael Caine's answer to Lolita, stops kidding round at the Ascot, City, tomorrow.

Stanley, the 1980s' answer to Alvin Purple, decamps from the Hoyts Centre tomorrow.

Deputy Leader. Mr Armstrong became National Party spokesman on agriculture while Mr Murray became spokesman on local government. What then are we to make of this: yesterday Mr Murray put out a press release about a plague of mice. Is this a comeback attempt? No doubt other party members are engaging in close textual analysis of his words:

"An incredible bureaucratic bungle is preventing much needed mice bait from being available to protect crops in NSW, Mr Wal Murray, MP...

Peats. Yesterday it was left to the Victorian Consumer Affairs Minister, Peter Spyker, to unveil the latest killer products. He announced that the Victorian Government had banned snaplock beads, Geri-bags, Magic Eggs and stuffed venomous snakes. Mr Spyker said small connecting pieces in the beads toy broke off easily and could be inhaled by a child. He said Geribags had been advertised as suitable for transporting petrol, but they could not be sealed, would not stand upright and were easily...

Next day, the English-language China Daily took up the story with a picture on the front page. Miss Sun was now "the first peasant in China to own a car." Then the official government news agency, Xinhua, offered this headline: "A new Japanese car — the first ever bought by a local peasant." The story said: "Sun Guiying will drive her silver Toyota around to make business contacts and promote egg sales."

...nese entrepreneur on ...pitalist running-board

...is point, foreign correspon-...went to interview Miss Sun. ...ey learned that the Toyota ...everal years old. It had been ...y the Japanese Embassy in ...and sold off to the only ...used car agency in the city, ...had resold it to Miss Sun at ...igher than the vehicle was ...new. When asked to demon-...he car, Miss Sun said she did ...ve a licence, she had never ...and she had no immediate ...o learn. Miss Sun's husband, ...Fuliang, then took the ...s of the car, now decorated ...arge plastic chicken perched ...dashboard. While attempting ...up to the garage, Mr Zhang ...corner of the family house, ...chips of masonry flying. ...ang then revealed that far ...eing a peasant, he worked as ...r official with the National ...'s Political Consultative ...ence, an advisory body to ...inese hierarchy. He said he ...e car to drive to work each ...the city, and to drop two of ...dren at their government ...he family not only has the ...t carpets, a color TV, and ...rniture. But Mr Zhang ...ised that he is a man of the ..."I'm not a capitalist, they ...people. I prefer to be called ...repreneur."

THE MAGIC STROP OIL AT BROADWAY AND WALL STREET.

...one else can afford to miss. As a special service to competitors, Radio Choice offers this handy hint from the Pee Wee Wilson Songbook: *Walk the plank, ride the hook, corner left and right and keep it nice and tight and, above all, keep your toes up on the nose.*

7.05 pm, 2BL, Credit Cards: Yes, they can open many doors for

noted sufferers as Linus from the Peanuts comic strip? As one afflicted with Papaphobia (fear of the Pope), I will be a keen listener to this week's About Children series.

dramatisation of old medieval mystery plays by David Buck, which concludes tonight in The Stereo Play. Redemption deals with the crucifixion and resurrection of Christ. Timothy West is the Prologue.

Doug Anderson

and King Streets, 29-47/b, 290 1312.
Open Thursday evening and Saturday morning.

063

Stay in Touch

All you need to know about yesterday and today, plus a few surprises. Edited by David Dale

Travel tips

This item will explain how you can obtain $12,720 worth of first class return air travel to Europe for just $2,544, a feat achieved by Neville and Jill Wran last week. No, you don't have to be Premier of NSW. The answer is: become a Qantas employee, rise to a senior position, go on leave of absence, and then get retrenched. Mrs Wran used to work for Qantas, and as one of the airline's three international relations managers, she and her immediate family were entitled to two return trips at one fifth of the normal fare within a period of six years. This applied even though Mrs Wran went on leave of absence in 1981 to do a university course, and in 1983 elected to accept retrenchment when Qantas was cutting staff. The fares, like most airline staff fares, were sold on a space-available basis only, which means the Wrans would have been asked to settle for business or even economy class if full fare paying passengers had bought all the 28 seats at the sharp end of the plane. As it happens, they were lucky.

Preservations

Two pairs of white-winged wood duck, descended from birds brought to Britain 10 years ago to save them from extinction, were flown to Bangkok eventually will be returned to their natural habitat. They were raised at the Wildfowl Trust, in the village of Slimbridge. A spokesman for the trust said there may now be fewer than 200 pairs of the white-winged wood duck, called spirit duck from their ghost-like, wailing call, left in the tropical forests of South-East Asia. Offspring of the birds flown to Bangkok eventually will be released into Thailand's Huai Kha Kheng Forest Sanctuary.

Going, going

Blame It On Rio, Michael Caine's answer to Lolita, stops kidding round at the Ascot, City, tomorrow.

Stanley, the 1980s' answer to Alvin Purple, decamps from the Hoyts Centre tomorrow.

Tender Mercies is cruelly terminated at the State Two tomorrow, showing that Oscars aren't the attractions they once were.

The Day After blows out of the Lyceum tomorrow.

The Castanets, comedy rockers and 60s nostalgists, go back to Newcastle on Friday after delighting the Trade Union Club (212 1188).

The Hot Bagels, three clever singers and comics who'd be accused of perpetuating racist stereotypes if they weren't Jewish, get cut off at the end of their season at Kinselas, Taylor Square, on Saturday (331 6200).

Bear Dinkum, the anarcho-terpsichorean koala, eats roots, and leaves the Sailors' Home Theatre, The Rocks, on Sunday. (27 3274).

What they did in Macquarie Street

We know Ron Mulock is back in Sydney running the State, but nobody seems to know for sure. Or care, actually. The interesting stuff is happening in the National Party. You will recall, of course, that immediately after the election, Wal Murray was defeated by Ian Armstrong in the party ballot for

Deputy Leader. Mr Armstrong became National Party spokesman on agriculture while Mr Murray became spokesman on local government. What then are we to make of this: yesterday Mr Murray put out a press release about a plague of mice. Is this a comeback attempt? No doubt other party members are engaging in close textual analysis of his words:

"An incredible bureaucratic bungle is preventing much needed mice bait from being available to protect crops in NSW, Mr Wal Murray, MP, Member for Barwon, said today. The bait, bromadioline, is available from the manufacturer, Rentokil Pty Ltd, but cannot be distributed because plastic bags with the correct printing in them are not available...'The Minister for Agriculture has now had 19 months to perfect a plastic bag to hold 15 kilograms of mixed bait — he has not bothered to do so . . . A mice plague in many towns will also spread disease and cause severe damage.'"

Music

St Matthew Passion at the Opera House from 8 pm; Marcia Hines at Didi's Bar, Brookvale, from 9 pm; Facial Expressions, a folk group from Alice Springs (so presumably the expressions are shock and horror) at Jerry Boam's Wine Bar, Miranda, from 8 pm; Western Youth Orchestra and Anthony Baldwin on piano do Rachmaninoff, Sibelius and Vivaldi from 7 pm at the Kings School, Parramatta; Soft Parade plus Bionic Louts at the Lismore Hotel, City, from 8 pm; Vulgar Beatmen plus Dugites at the Blue Gum Hotel, Waitara, from 7 pm; Radio Therapy at the Epping Hotel from 8 pm; Alter Ego plus No Drama at the Strawberry Hill Hotel, Surry Hills, from 8 pm; Oz Born Bros at Sheila's, North Sydney, from 9 pm.

Novelties

Paul Landa, Australia's foremost campaigner against consumer ripoffs and health risks before the State election, has gone strangely quiet since gaining the safe seat of

Peats. Yesterday it was left to the Victorian Consumer Affairs Minister, Peter Spyker, to unveil the latest killer products. He announced that the Victorian Government had banned snaplock beads, Geri-bags, Magic Eggs and stuffed venomous snakes. Mr Spyker said small connecting pieces in the beads toy broke off easily and could be inhaled by a child. He said Geribags had been advertised as suitable for transporting petrol, but they could not be sealed, would not stand upright and were easily punctured. Stuffed venomous snakes which had not had their venom glands, ducts and fangs removed were dangerous because of the possibility of lingering poison. And Magic Eggs, which are small plastic novelties which expand when immersed in water, had been put under a temporary ban while tests were made to determine whether the toy could swell in the digestive system if swallowed.

Great moments in media

The Chinese media, being government controlled, does not sensationalise. Except sometimes. Mark Baker, this column's field agent in Peking, has sent us this report on how China is emulating the West:

Last month the Chinese media devoted a lot of space to the story of how Sun Guiying, the nation's leading chicken farmer, bought a car. It had almost everything the Chinese press loves — success through toil, use of technology in economic modernisation, even female equality. Miss Sun, of Beiqijia commune on the outskirts of Peking, was reported to have paid the equivalent of $4,800 for a Toyota car after reaping a profit of $19,170 last year from her poultry business. She and her family were photographed posing like lottery winners beside the car. "The family is the first to have ever purchased a car in the suburbs of Peking," said the Peking Daily. "This year she sold 32,000 kilograms of eggs to the State. But having got rich herself, she never forgot the collective and this year deposited 7000 yuan ($3,630) with the production brigade."

Next day, the English-language China Daily took up the story with a picture on the front page. Miss Sun was now "the first peasant in China to own a car." Then the official government news agency, Xinhua, offered this headline: "A new Japanese car — the first ever bought by a local peasant." The story said: "Sun Guiying will drive her silver Toyota around to make business contacts and promote egg sales."

Chinese entrepreneur on capitalist running-board

At this point, foreign correspondents went to interview Miss Sun. First they learned that the Toyota was several years old. It had been used by the Japanese Embassy in Peking and sold off to the only official used car agency in the city, which had resold it to Miss Sun at a price higher than the vehicle was worth new. When asked to demonstrate the car, Miss Sun said she did not have a licence, she had never driven and she had no immediate plans to learn. Miss Sun's husband, Zhang Fulieng, then took the controls of the car, now decorated with a large plastic chicken perched on the dashboard. While attempting to back up to the garage, Mr Zhang hit the corner of the family house, sending chips of masonry flying. Mr Zhang then revealed that far from being a peasant, he worked as a senior official with the National People's Political Consultative Conference, an advisory body to the Chinese hierarchy. He said he used the car to drive to work each day in the city, and to drop two of his children at their government jobs. The family not only has the car, but carpets, a color TV, and new furniture. But Mr Zhang emphasised that he is a man of the people: "I'm not a capitalist, they exploit people. I prefer to be called an entrepreneur."

TELEVISION CHOICE

Movie: Diary of a Madman (1963), 10 at noon: Having sorted out the weeds in his garden, Vincent Price turns his attention to this little number based on a short story by Guy de Maupassant. Vincent is cast as a French judge possessed by a demon. Great scope for pursing of the lips and rolling of the eyes.

Our World: Everest, the Last Unclaimed Ridge, 2 at 7.30 pm: The expedition on which this doco is based took place in 1982. A British team decided to claim Mt Everest from the north along a ridge that had never been claimed before. At first everything went smoothly for the claimbers and the view from the ridge was sublaime. Then tragedy struck, as it tends to do on these expeditions,

and the cameraman, Joe Tasker, and Peter Boardmen suddenly vanished.

Dynasty: The Bungalow, 9 at 8.30 pm: With Jeff in control of Colbyco, Adam looks around for a new power base. Blake is peeved that Krystle is sure Mark didn't set the cabin on fire. Alexis, quite understandably, is a little jittery that a killer is stalking her person.

Movie: Persons Unknown (1958), 0/28 at 8.30 pm: Some of Italy's best comic actors combine their talents for this one about a bungled safe-napping raid on a pawn shop. Stars Claudia Cardinale and Marcello Mastroianni.

Comedy Video Story, 2 at 11 pm: This show presents practitioners of the "new wave" stand-up comedians who give cleaned-up

versions of their club and pub routines. In between acts are pop music clips. Tonight's starters are Rodney Rude, Keith Scott, David Cotter and George Smilovici. If you like your stand-up comedians in stereo, you can listen to the sound on 2JJJ-FM.

Movie: Twenty-three Paces to Baker Street (1956), 9 at midnight: A scare a minute with Van Johnson, Vera Miles and Cecil Parker. Concerns a blind man's struggle to nab a murderer.

Dallas: The Oil Baron's Ball, 10 at 9.30 pm: With Ray's murder trial over, the Ewings decide to unwind at the Oil Baron's Ball. Priscilla Presley sets out to demonstrate she's not just a well-connected surname.

Richard Coleman

RADIO CHOICE

TALK

8.15 am, 2JJJ-FM, Surfing with Edgar Allen Chamberpot:
Hear the loud alarum bells,
Brazen bells,
How they clang and clash and roar —
What horror they outpour
On the bosom of the palpitating air
. . . How true! Andrew McKinnon braves the palpitating air of Bells Beach for the annual surf classic. Tom Carroll doesn't have to be there now, but it's an event that no one else can afford to miss. As a special service to competitors, Radio Choice offers this handy hint from the Pee Wee Wilson Songbook: *Walk the plank, ride the hook, corner left and right and keep it nice and tight and, above all, keep your toes up on the nose,*

Surfer Joes. Heh, heh!

11.15 am, 2FC, Fear and Loathing in Children: What do children fear? Is the Bogeyman still a force to be reckoned with? Can facial features become frozen into hideous stone visages by sudden shifts of the wind? And where are the serpents of yesteryear which used to leap from cracks in the pavement to strike at young ankles? More to the point, how do phobias such as pantophobia, the fear of everything, strike such noted sufferers as Linus from the Peanuts comic strip? As one afflicted with Papaphobia (fear of the Pope), I will be a keen listener to this week's About Children series.

7.05 pm, 2BL, Credit Cards: Yes, they can open many doors for

you — literally — and make you like the Queen. You need never carry real cash if you belong to the plastic society. Think of all the vending machine temptations you can resist. Representatives from the Bankcard Association of Australia and American Express man the open line in tonight's edition of The Bob Hudson Show.

PLAY

8 pm, ABC-FM, The Image of God is not a new album by Michael Jackson. It's a five-part dramatisation of old medieval mystery plays by David Buck, which concludes tonight in The Stereo Play. Redemption deals with the crucifixion and resurrection of Christ. Timothy West is the Prologue.

Doug Anderson

It's bunnykins birthday time at Shorters. Join the party at Shorters and Royal Doulton celebrate 50 years of Bunnykins Magic. Figures, eggcups, baby plates, special two hundred mugs, tea cups and much more together in a very special display at Shorters now.

Shorters

193 Clarence Street, Sydney. Between Market and King Streets. 29 4476, 290 1312. Open Thursday evening and Saturday morning.

The highway is like a lion's mouth (video stills), 2018

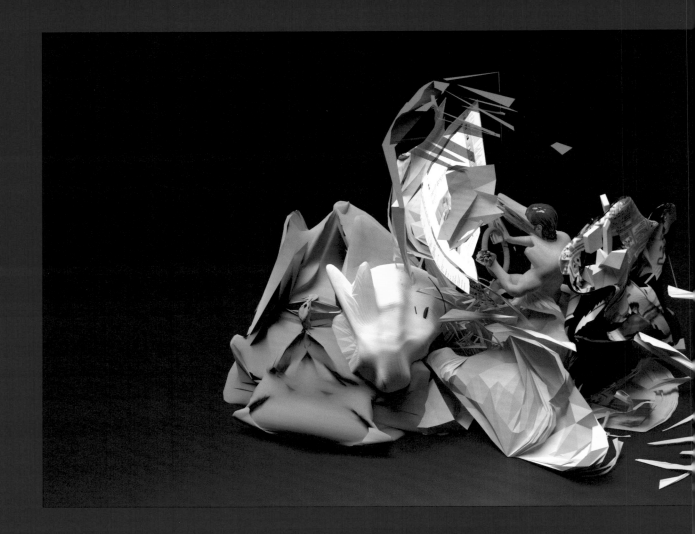

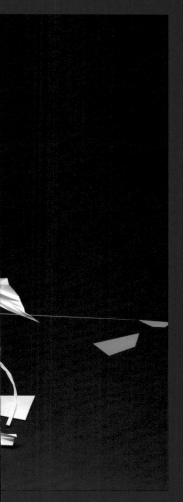

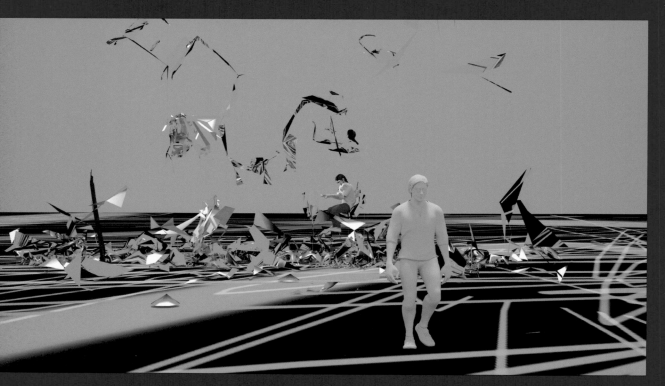

mobile
off
seat belt
ON

十字路口
生死關
遵守規則
保命符

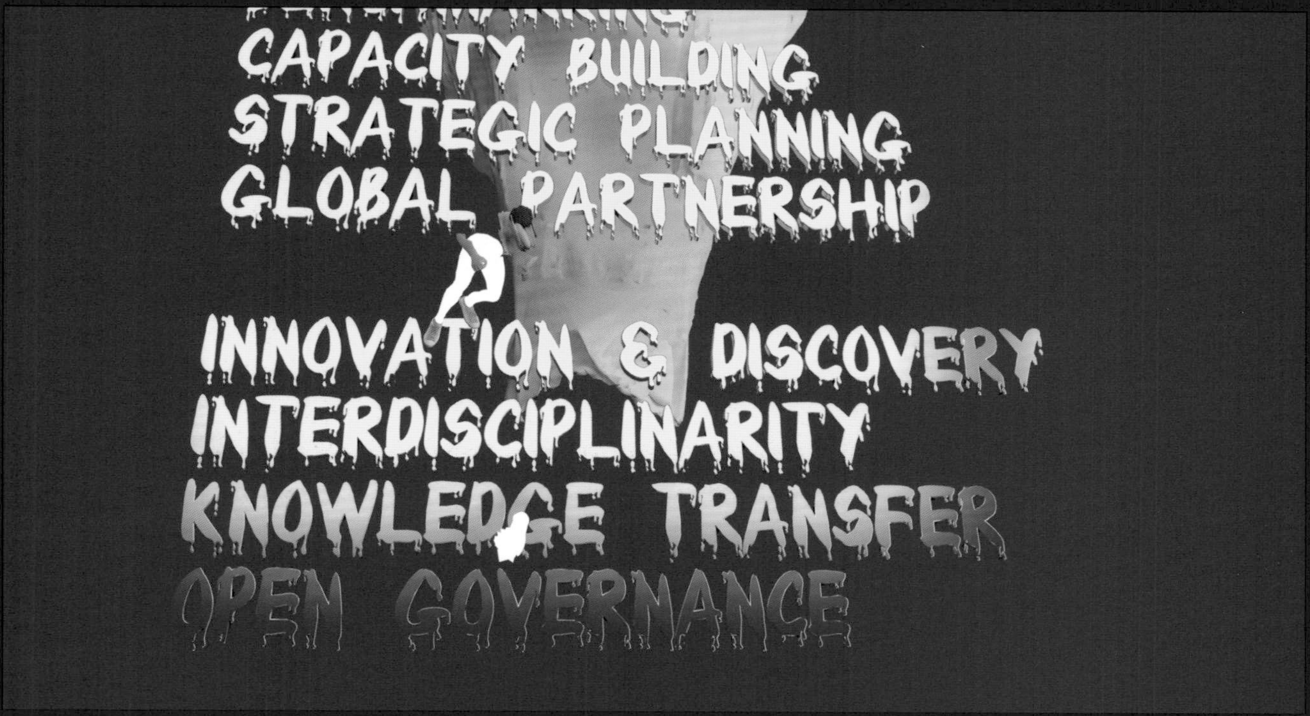

CAPACITY BUILDING
STRATEGIC PLANNING
GLOBAL PARTNERSHIP

INNOVATION & DISCOVERY
INTERDISCIPLINARITY
KNOWLEDGE TRANSFER
OPEN GOVERNANCE

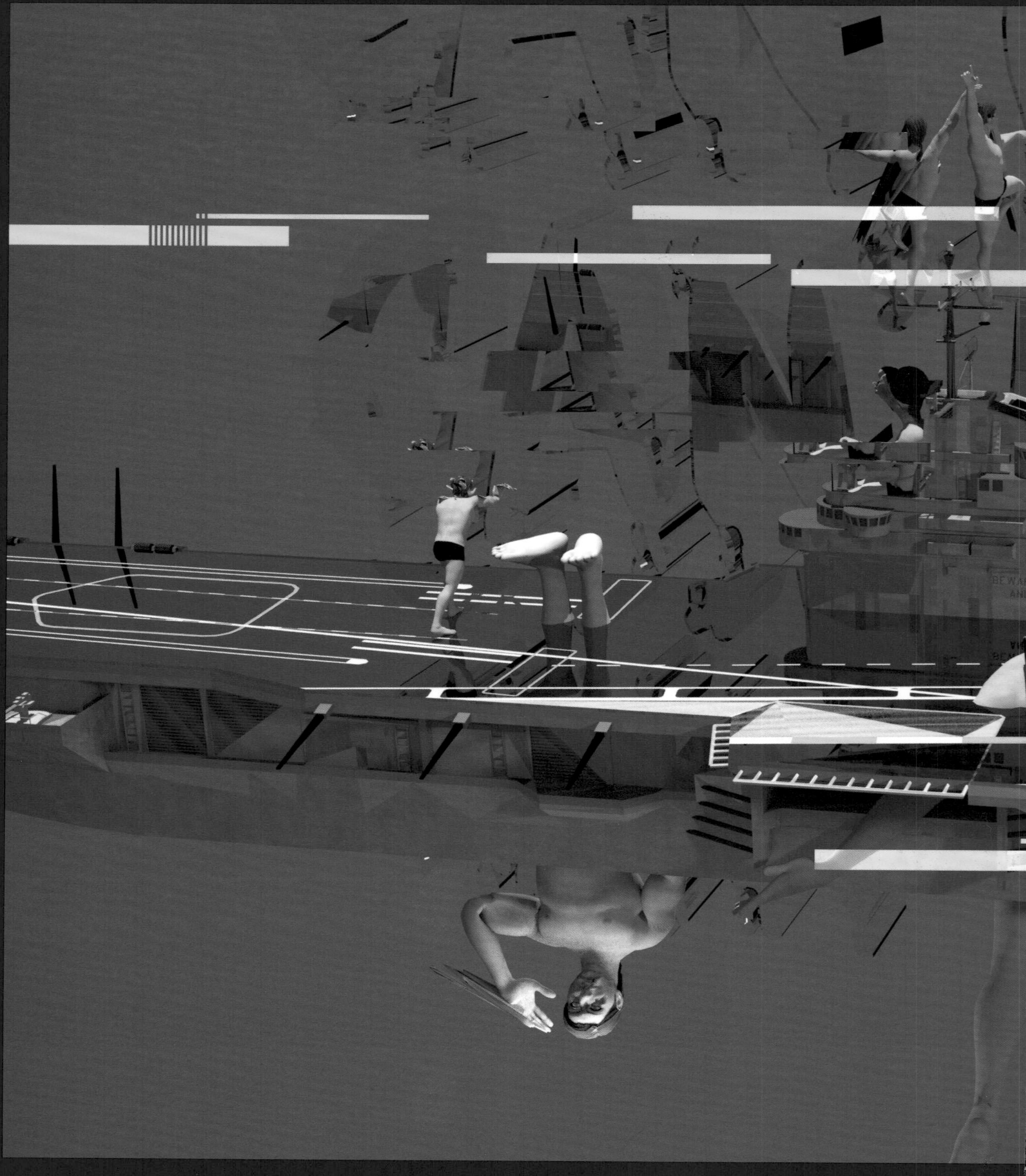

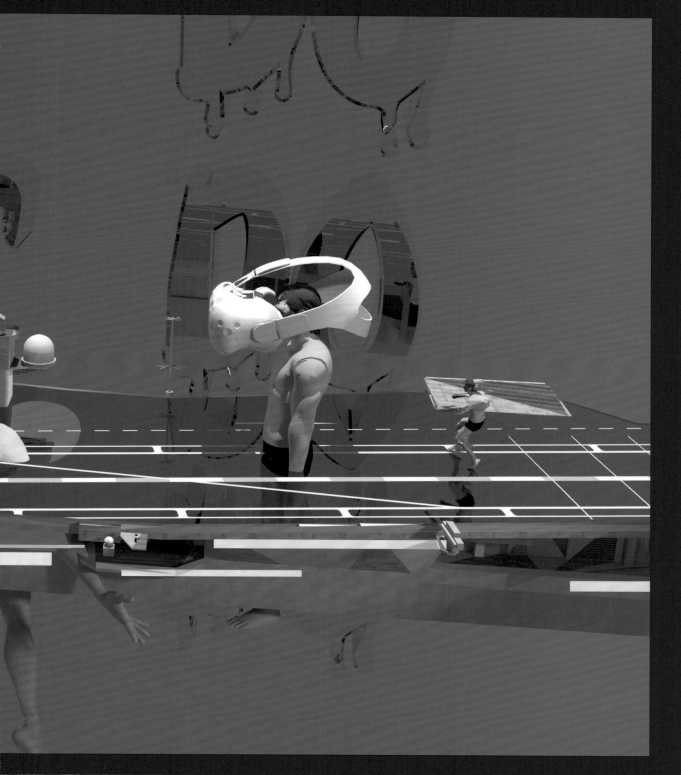

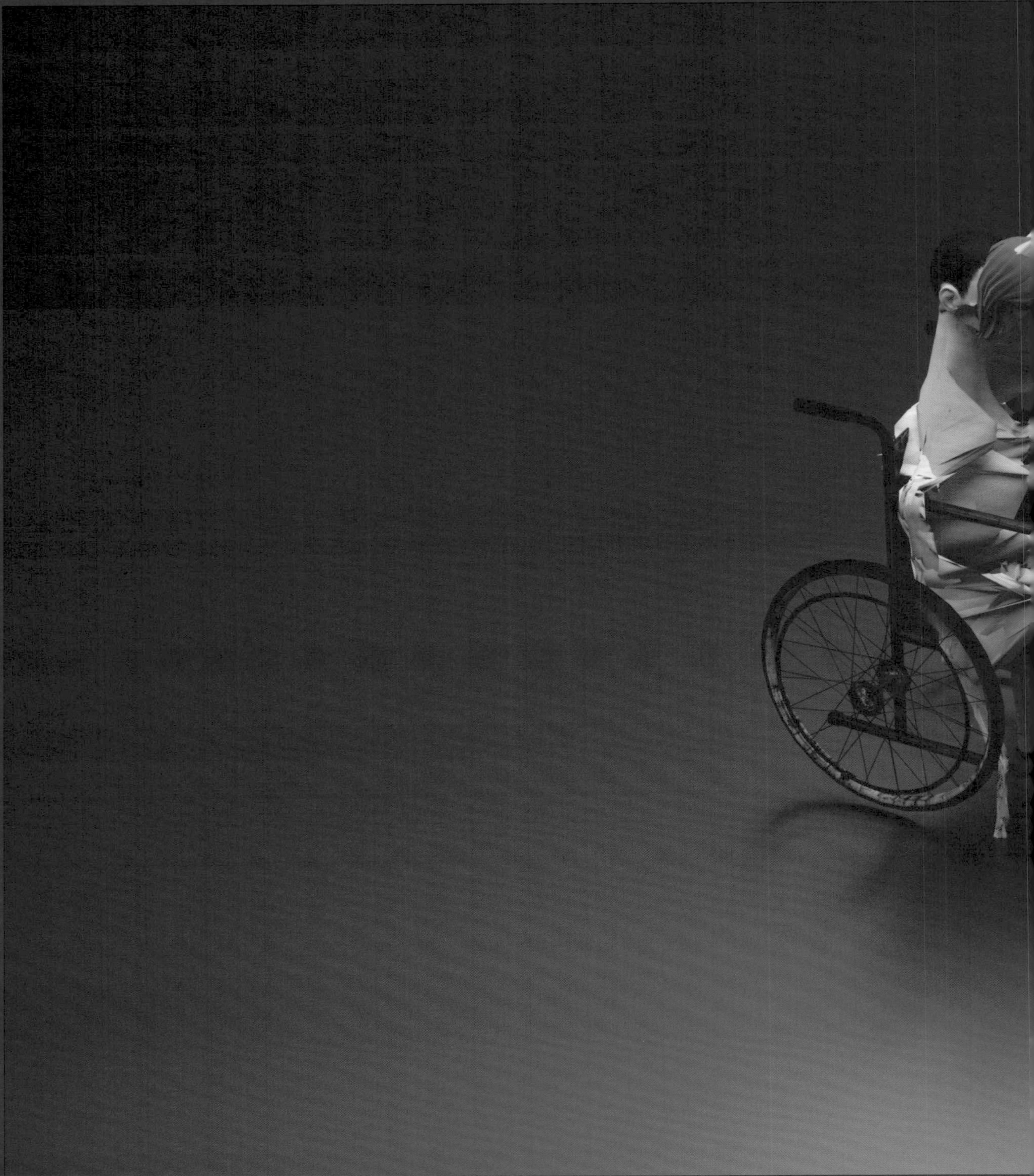

My car makes noises 17 (squealing is very linear), 2018. Ink, colored pencil, and soft pastel on paper, 11 3/4 x 8 1/4 in. (30 x 21 cm)

My car makes noises 6 (a pencil pusher with the pencil pusher blues), 2018. Ink, colored pencil, and pastel on paper, 11 3/4 x 8 1/4 in. (30 x 21 cm)

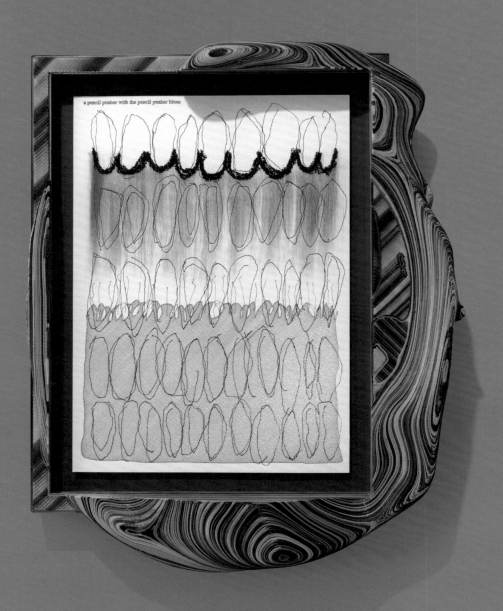

My car makes noises 7 (angry birds), 2018. Ink, colored pencil, and pastel on paper,
11 3/4 x 8 1/4 in. (30 x 21 cm)

My car makes noises 9 (bllgh blllgggh blllllgggghh), 2018. Ink, colored pencil, and pastel on paper, 11 3/4 x 8 1/4 in. (30 x 21 cm)

My car makes noises 16 (thud), 2018. Ink, colored pencil, and pastel on paper,
11 3/4 x 8 1/4 in. (30 x 21 cm)

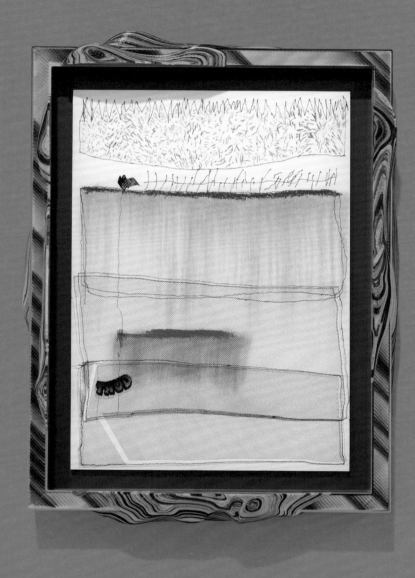

My car makes noises (show me the bones under the floor in your room), 2018. Ink,
colored pencil, and pastel on paper, 11 3/4 x 8 1/4 in. (30 x 21 cm)

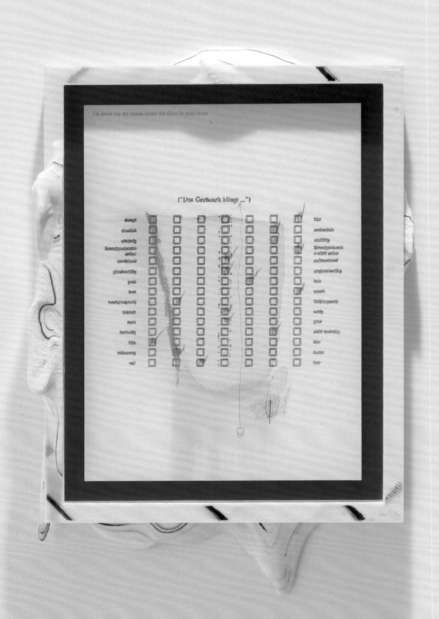

Interior pages of the booklet *Your Car as You Would Build It*, published by General Motors Company, 1934. Research material for *The highway is like a lion's mouth*, 2018

10

S E A T   C U S H I O N S

What is your preference?

CHECK ✓ ANSWER

☐ NARROW PIPING   ☐ WIDE PIPING

☐ PANEL TYPE   ☐ FLAT TRIM

☐ LOOSELY PADDED —OR— ☐ HEAVILY PADDED

"The Motorist of today not only likes to travel far and fast - but he expects his travel to be tireless, free from worry and nervous fatigue."

11

-just skip anything that doesn't interest you.

COLOR AND SHADE

Color of your <u>PRESENT</u> car ?

☐ BLACK   ☐ GRAY   ☐ GREEN

☐ BLUE   ☐ BROWN   ☐ RED

Color desired on your <u>NEXT</u> car ?

☐ BLACK   ☐ GRAY   ☐ GREEN

☐ BLUE   ☐ BROWN   ☐ RED

☐ LIGHT SHADE?   ☐ DARK SHADE?

HIGHLY POLISHED TRIMMINGS

What is your preference?

☐ Lots of Chromium plating ?   ☐ Restrained use of Chromium ?

☐ Don't Care

Chinese Immigration Service registration card for Won Alexander Cumyow, issued by Department of Immigration and Colonization, Dominion of Canada, 1924. Research material for *Da Da Company*, 2019

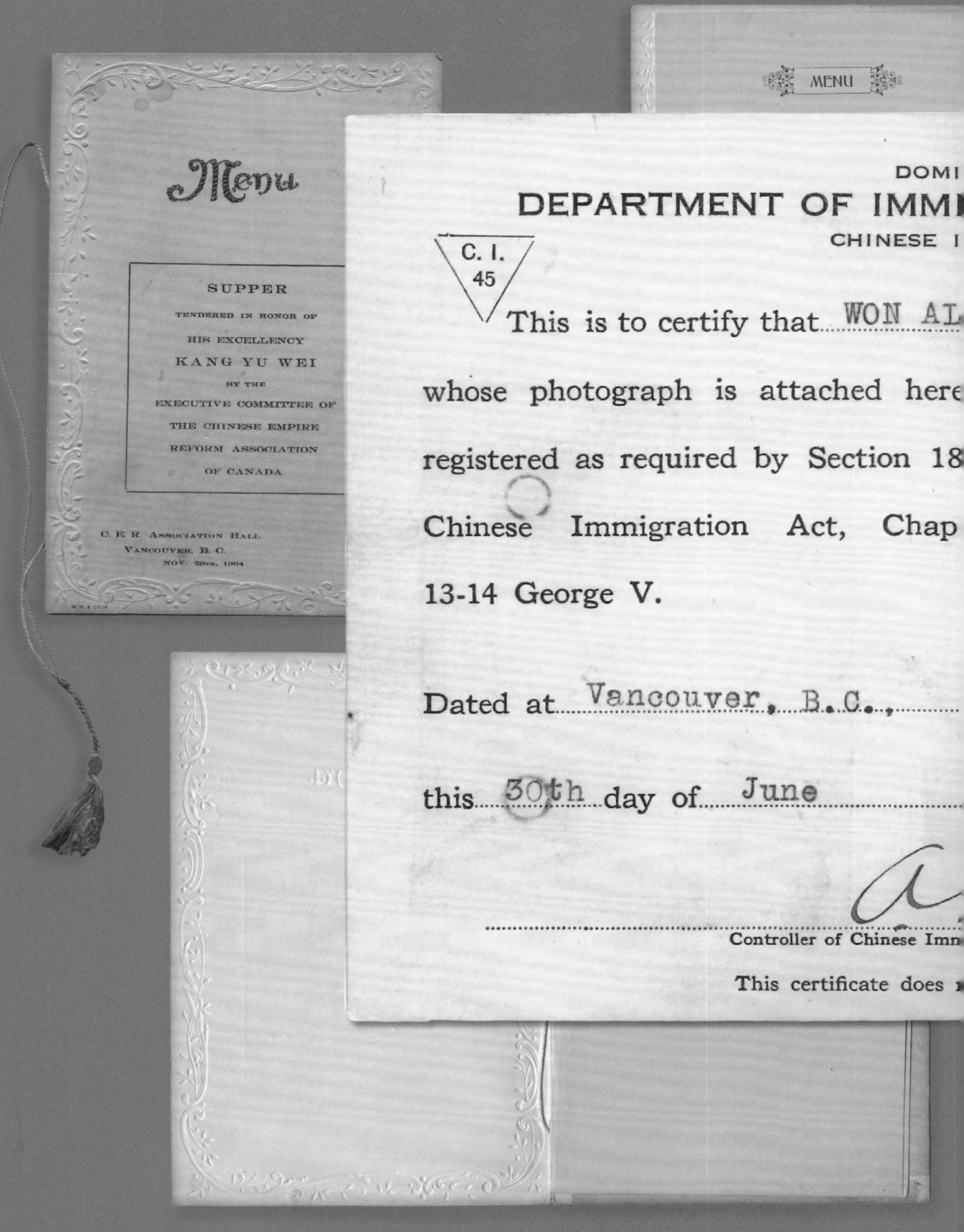

Menu

SUPPER

TENDERED IN HONOR OF

HIS EXCELLENCY

KANG YU WEI

BY THE

EXECUTIVE COMMITTEE OF

THE CHINESE EMPIRE

REFORM ASSOCIATION

OF CANADA

C. E. R. ASSOCIATION HALL

VANCOUVER, B. C.

NOV. 29TH, 1904

MENU

DOMI

DEPARTMENT OF IMM

CHINESE I

C. I.
45

This is to certify that WON AL

whose photograph is attached here

registered as required by Section 18

Chinese Immigration Act, Chap

13-14 George V.

Dated at Vancouver, B.C.,

this 30th day of June

Controller of Chinese Imm

This certificate does

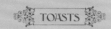

TOASTS

OF CANADA

TION AND COLONIZATION

ATION SERVICE

No. 52779

DER CUMYOW

lish legal status in Canada.

News-Advertiser, Camble St.

Supper menu in honor of Kang Yuwei, Executive Committee of the Chinese Empire Reform Association of Canada, Vancouver, 1904. Research material for *Da Da Company*, 2019

Menu

SUPPER

TENDERED IN HONOR OF

HIS EXCELLENCY

KANG YU WEI

BY THE

EXECUTIVE COMMITTEE OF

THE CHINESE EMPIRE

REFORM ASSOCIATION

OF CANADA

C. E. R. ASSOCIATION HALL
VANCOUVER, B. C.
NOV. 29TH, 1904

M. W. & CE LF   772F

DEPAR

C. I.
45

This is t

whose photogr

egistered as r

Chinese Imm

3-14 George V.

MENU

Gai Yung Yin Wo—Birdsnest Soup
Hong Yon Gai Kow—Almond Chicken
Gai Yung Yee Chee—Shark's Fins
Chow Wo Yung Har—Shrimp Omelette
Moo Goo Gai—Mushroom Chicken
Gai Chop Suey—Chicken Chop Suey
Chow Gai See Mein—Fried Noodles

DESSERT

Chow Heong Jew—Fried Banana
Chow Hong Yun—Baked Almonds
Soon Kheong—Pickled Ginger
Tong Kheong—Preserved Ginger
Lai Chee—Lai Chee Nuts

PASTRY

Tong Bow Jai—Gai Daun Goo
Soong Goo

Kong Yun Wo—Almond Cream
Assorted Fruit

Suey San Cha—Suey Sen Tea

TOASTS

The King

The Emperor of China

The Emperor of Japan

The President of the United States

OUR GUEST

The Chinese Empire Reform Association

Our Other Guests

The Press

The Ladies

...NIZATION

No............52

Inside
Stanley
Park

News-Advertiser, Cambie St.

...lish le...

EXECUTIVE COMMITTEE

C. YIP YEN
W. A. CUMYOW
YIP SANG
MARK LONG
YIP ON
HO JUN CHONG
YIP QUONG
CHIN MING POO
CHU HONG
LAW S. YAM

Da Da Company (work-in-progress documentation), 3D rendering of Won Alexander Cumyow, 2019

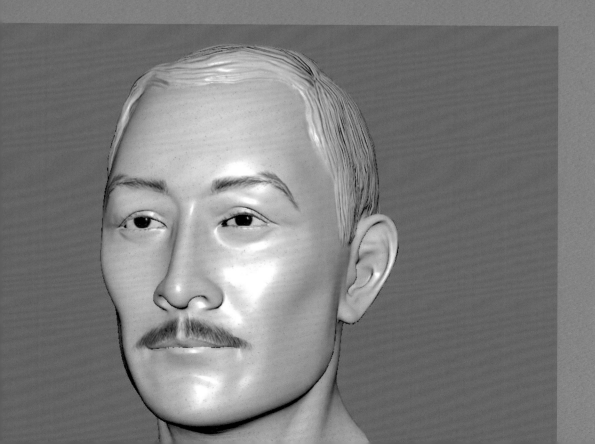

Member portraits of the Chinese Empire Reform Association of Canada, date unknown. Research material for *Da Da Company*, 2019

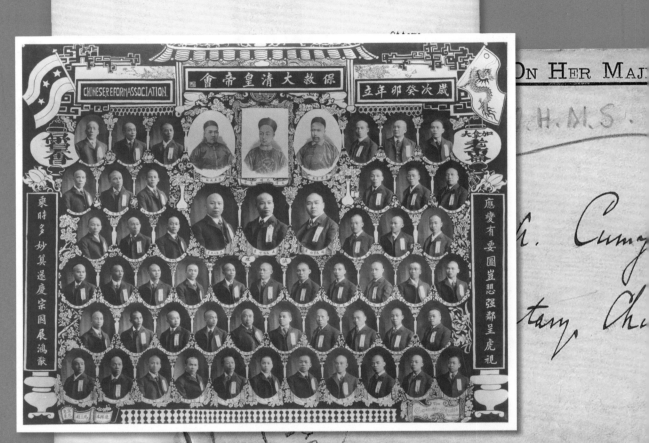

W.A.Cumyow, Esq.
Secretary Chinese Reform Association,
Vancouver, B.C.

Portrait of Won Alexander Cumyow's family, date unknown. Research material for
Da Da Company, 2019

Envelope to Won Alexander Cumyow from the Governor General's Secretary, Ottawa, 1900. Research material for *Da Da Company*, 2019

Ottawa,

ON HER MAJ

O.H.M.S.

W. A. Cumy

Secretary, Chi

W.A.Cumyow, Esq.
Secretary Chinese Reform Association,
Vancouver, B.C.

Property of
(Mrs.) Hilda Lanyon
3093 W. 2nd Ave
Vanc. B.C

s SERVICE.

Sir,

Reform Association

Vancouver

B.C.

5
OTTAWA
JUL 11
00
FREE

Letter to Won Alexander Cumyow from the Governor General's Secretary, Ottawa, acknowledging receipt of the Chinese Empire Reform Association of Canada's petition, 1900. Research material for *Da Da Company*, 2019

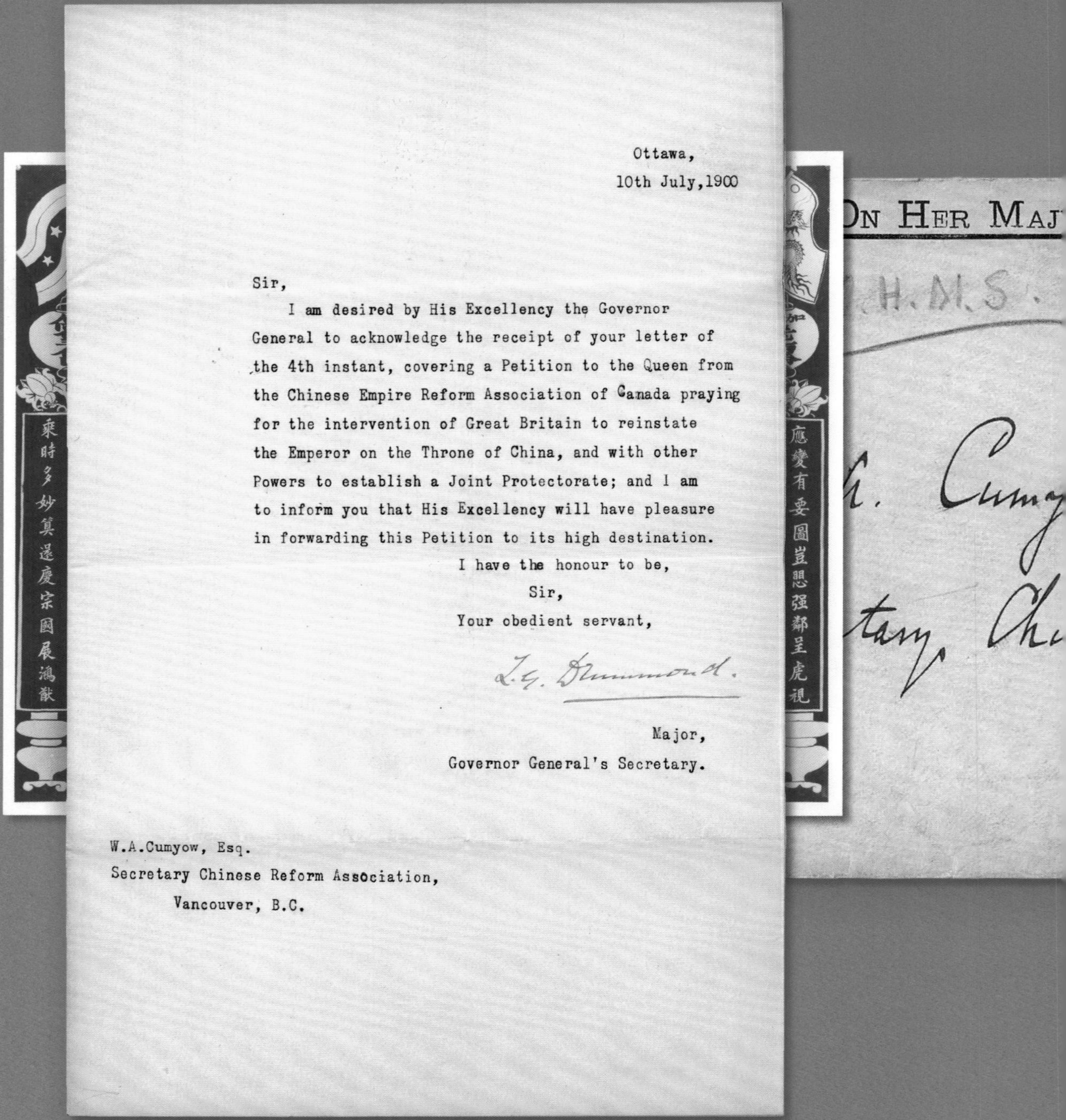

Ottawa,
10th July,1900

Sir,

I am desired by His Excellency the Governor General to acknowledge the receipt of your letter of the 4th instant, covering a Petition to the Queen from the Chinese Empire Reform Association of Canada praying for the intervention of Great Britain to reinstate the Emperor on the Throne of China, and with other Powers to establish a Joint Protectorate; and I am to inform you that His Excellency will have pleasure in forwarding this Petition to its high destination.

I have the honour to be,

Sir,

Your obedient servant,

L.G. Drummond.

Major,
Governor General's Secretary.

W.A.Cumyow, Esq.
Secretary Chinese Reform Association,
Vancouver, B.C.

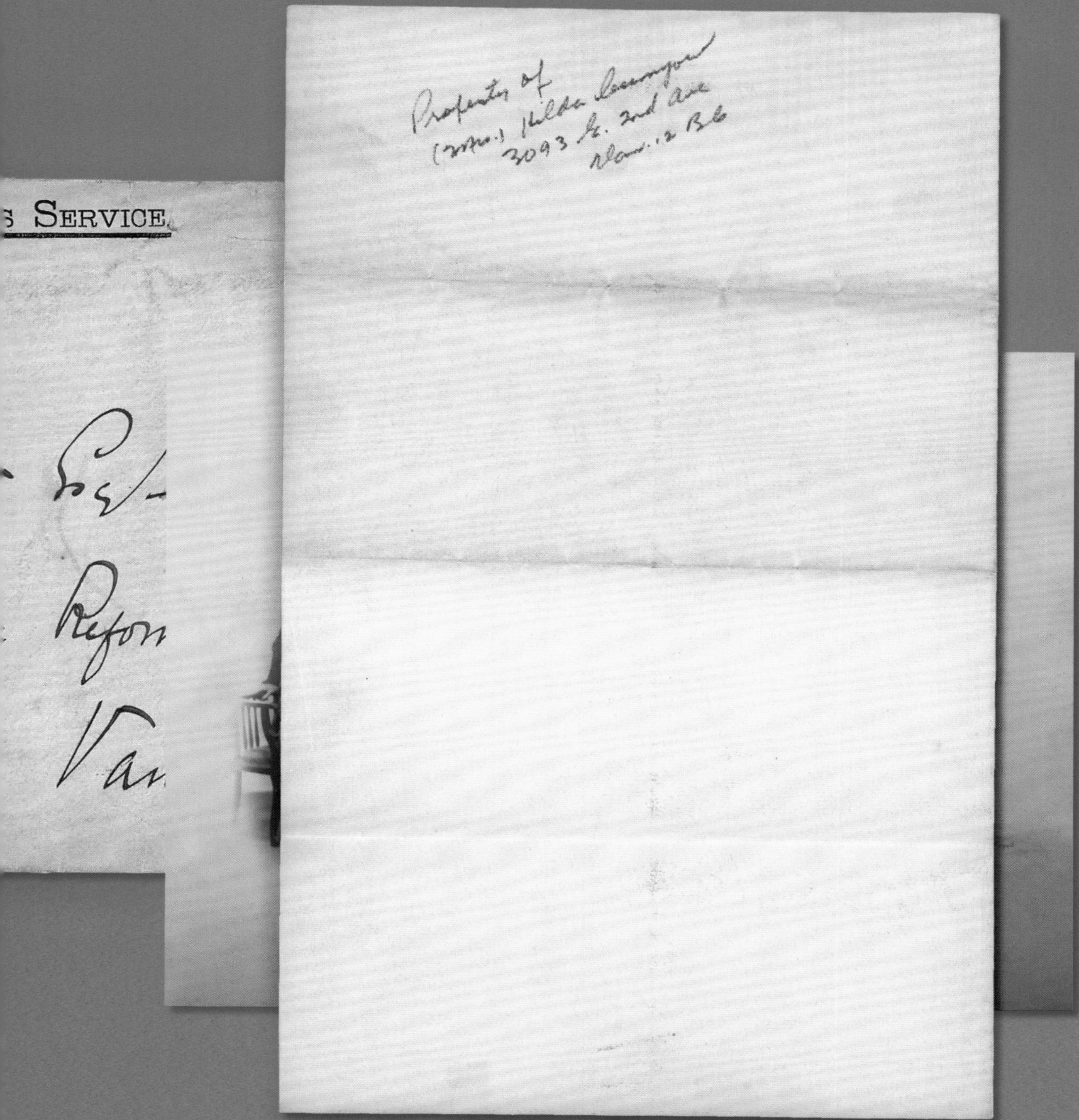

Property of
(Mrs.) Hilda Lumpson
3093 E. 2nd Ave
Van. 12 BC

SERVICE

Lol~

Refor

Van

Bottomless fountains of rose-scented coffee

These are a few of my favourite sins

American emperor and monarchs of England

American emperor and monarchs of England

These are a few things I won won won won won won!

When I'm eating cake

Gods of the free world and rulers in Eden

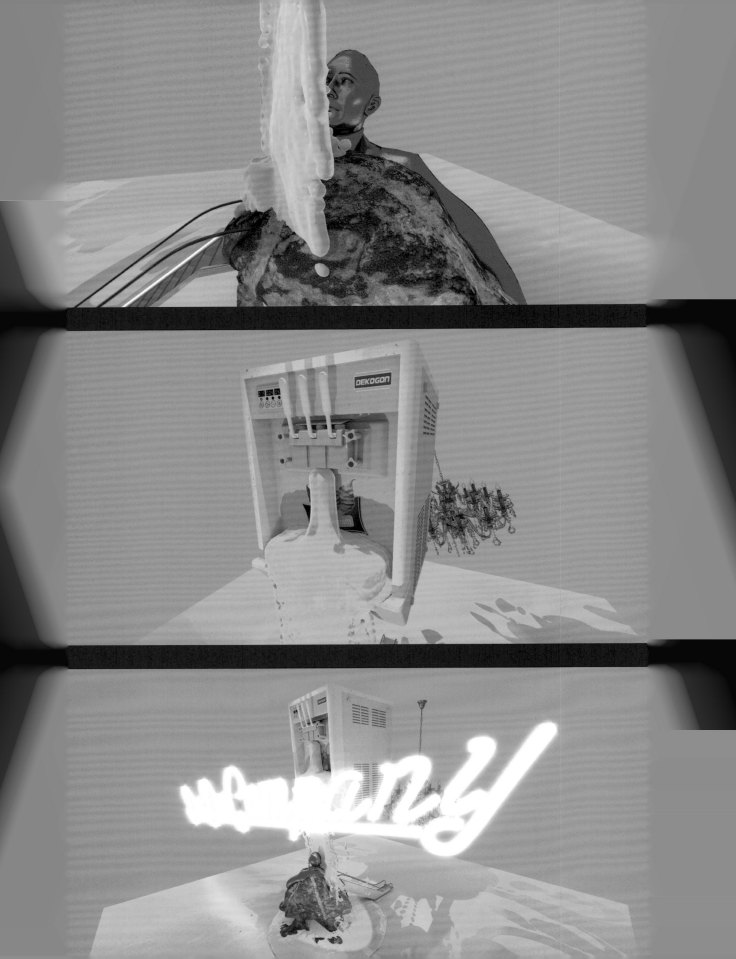

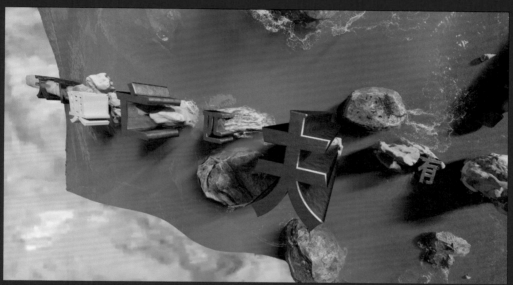

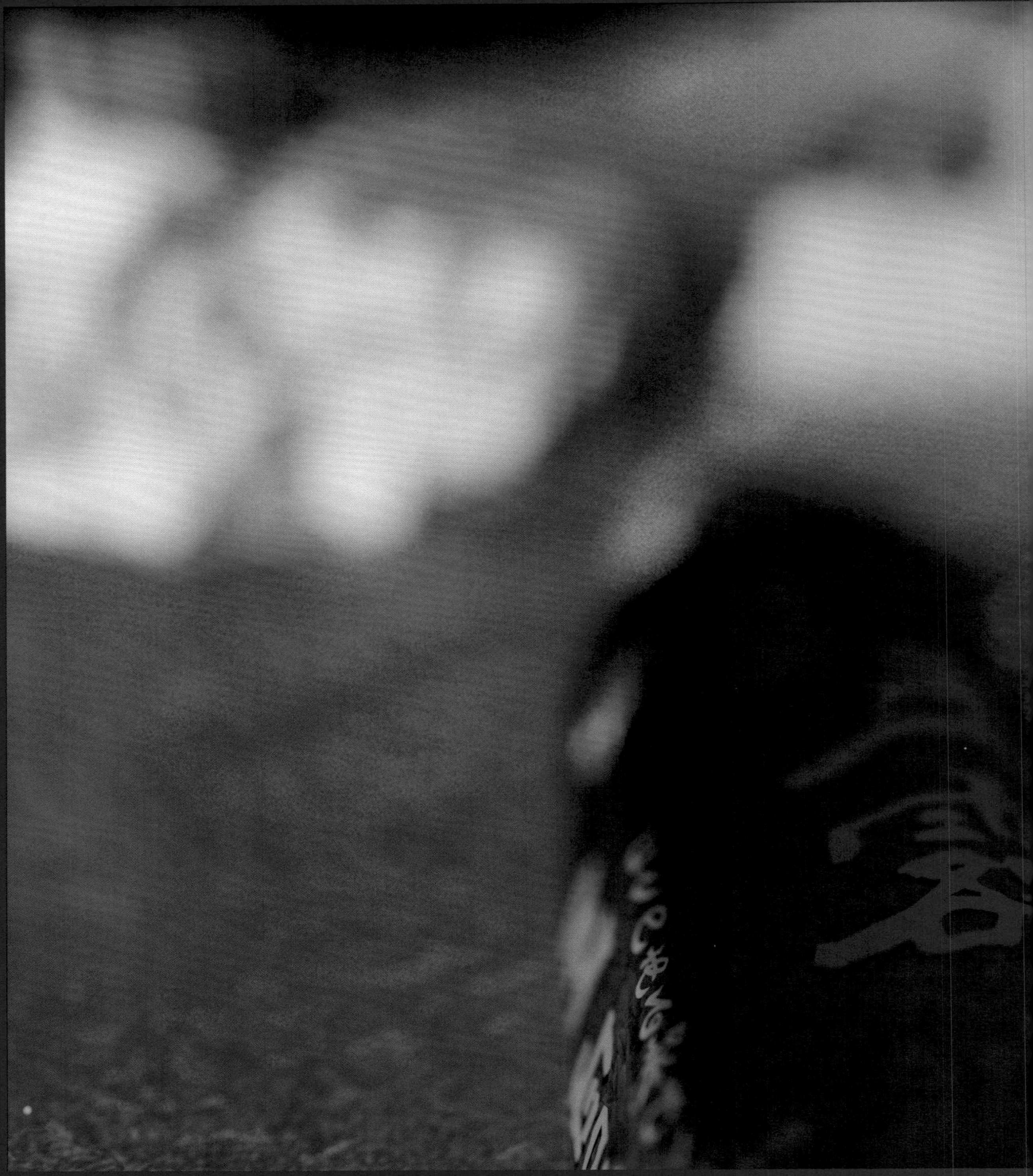

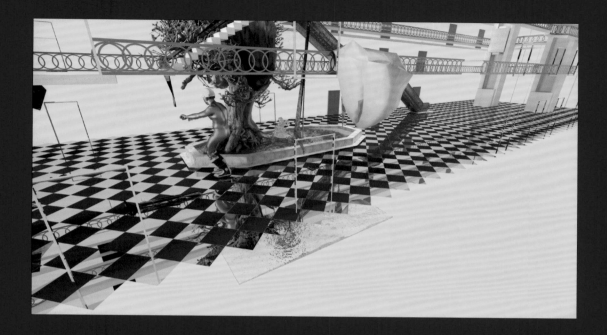

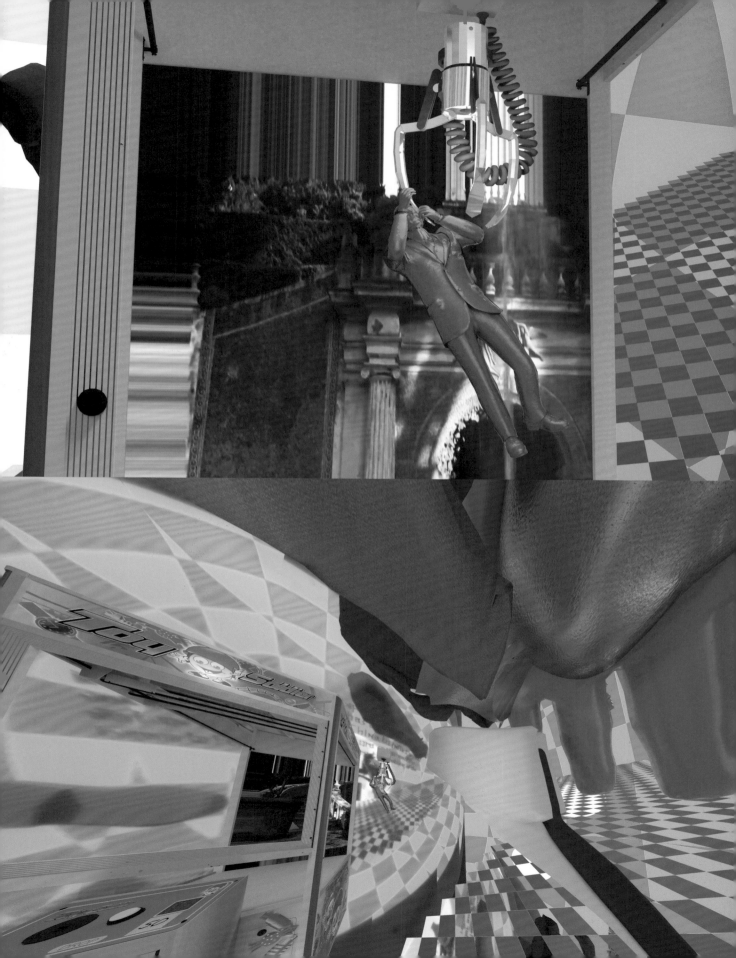

(Man's voice over the radio): I have seen people change

To extend the longevity of joy

Let me see the wonderful otherlands of the world
So I may be glad forever, and my heart would be filled with joy!

AV

(Lead): It's a heaven over there! / Where is heaven?
(Chorus): Singapore!

AV

Let me see the wonderful otherlands of the world

City Garden, 2019. C-prints on archival paper, each: 6 1/8 x 10 in. (15.5 x 25.5 cm)

City Garden (aquarium and cramp school), 2019. C-print, lightbox, 30 x 19 3/4 x 4 3/4 in. (76 x 50 x 12 cm)

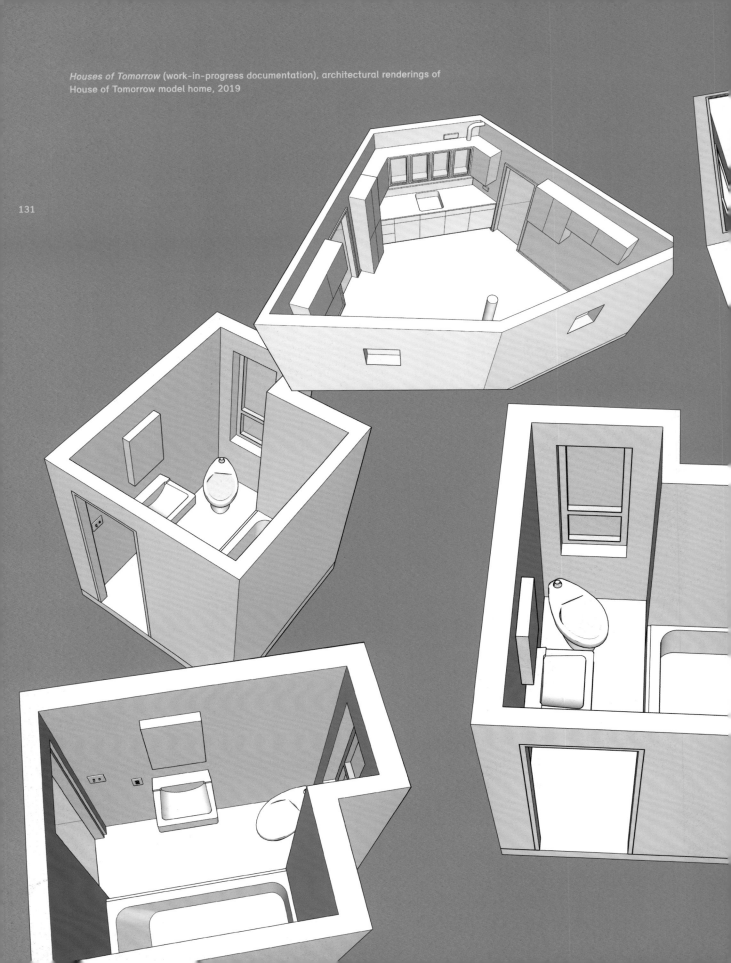

Houses of Tomorrow (work-in-progress documentation), architectural renderings of
House of Tomorrow model home, 2019

133

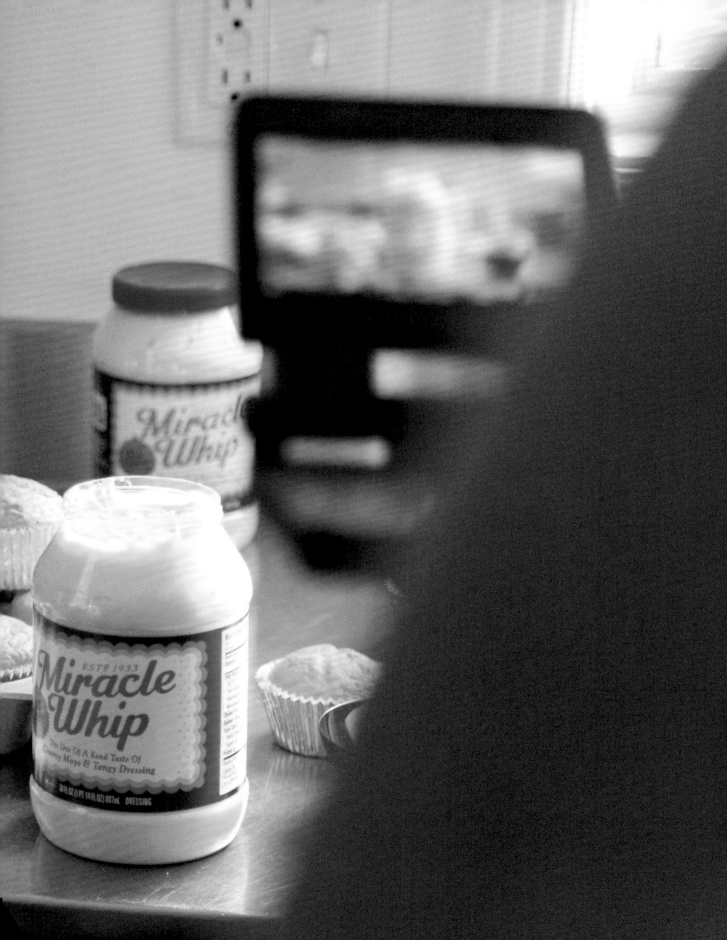

Houses of Tomorrow (video stills), 2019

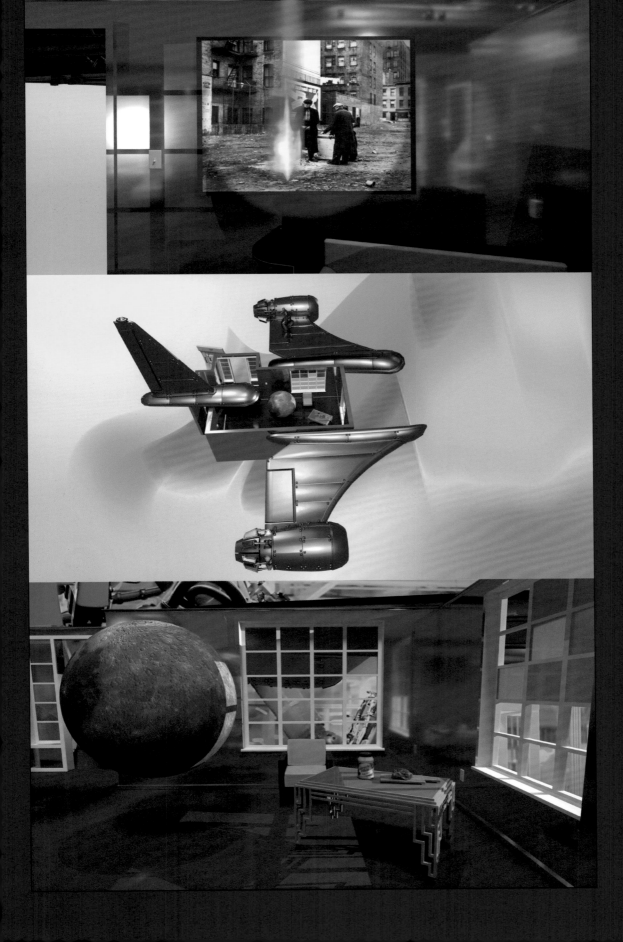

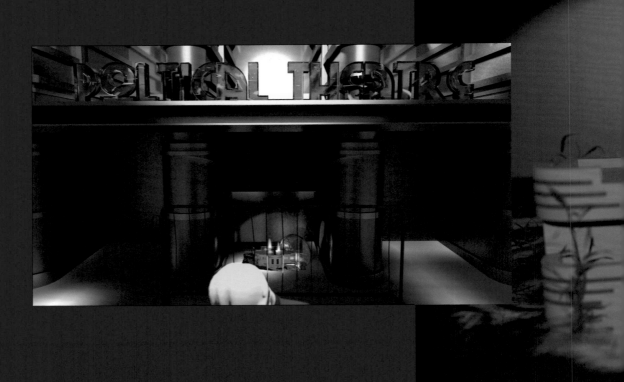

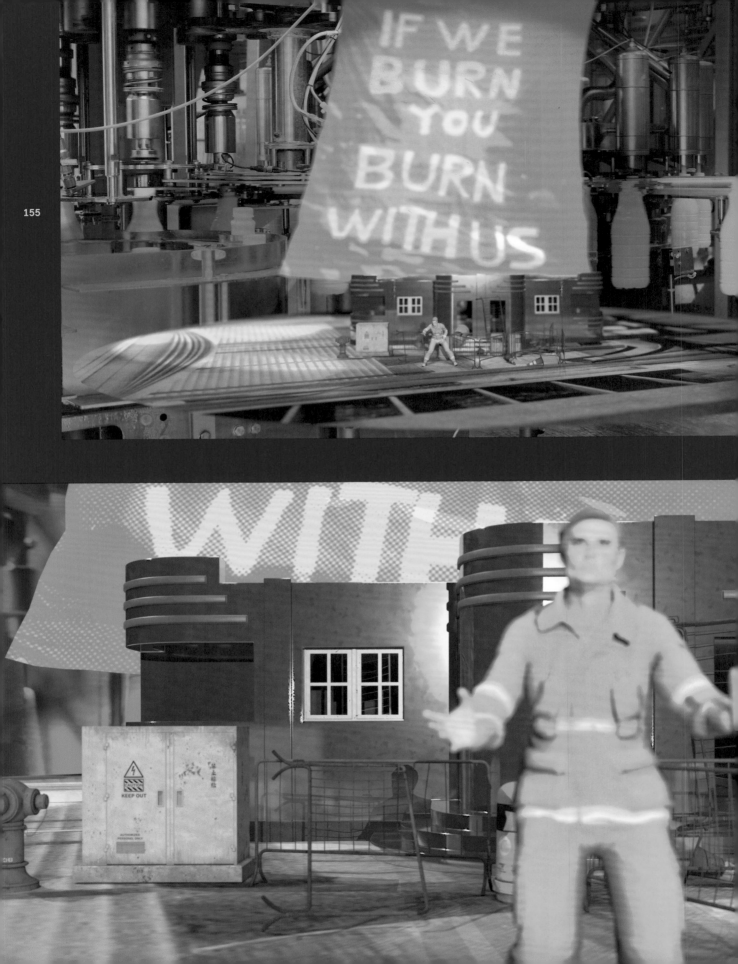

Plaster sculptures from Malvina Hoffman's *Races of Mankind* project, 1930s, from left: Chao Te An, student from northern China; Dr. Hu Shih, from eastern China; and Ah Ying, Cantonese woman from Hong Kong. The Field Museum, Chicago. Research material for *Houses of Tomorrow*, 2019

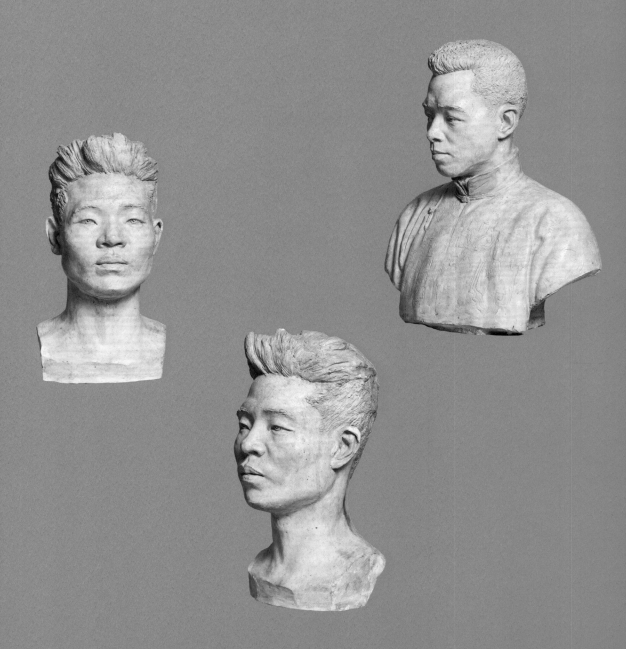

Bronze sculptures from Malvina Hoffman's *Races of Mankind* project, 1930s, from left: Dr. Weng Wenhao, man from southern China; Ma Yu Lin, Chinese man; and Gedung, Mongolian man. The Field Museum, Chicago. Research material for *Houses of Tomorrow*, 2019

165

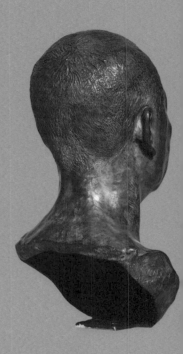

Production documentation of *The world falls apart into facts #2 (The Dream Seller by E. Markham Lee as performed by the Chinese University of Hong Kong Chorus)*, 2019

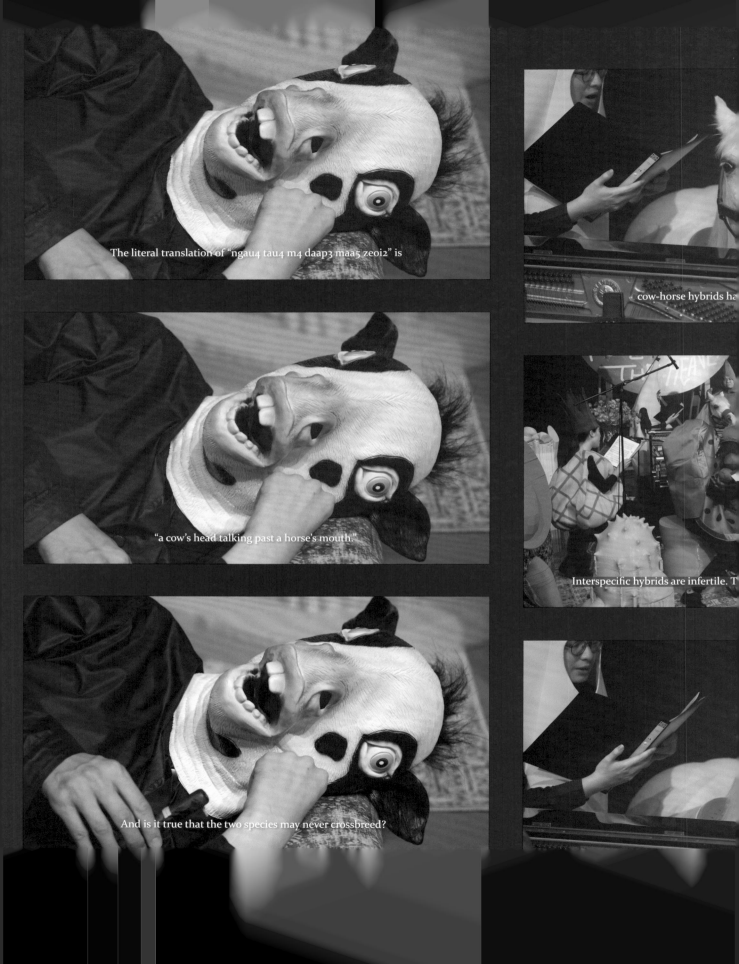

The literal translation of "ngau4 tau4 m4 daap3 maa5 zeoi2" is

"a cow's head talking past a horse's mouth."

And is it true that the two species may never crossbreed?

cow-horse hybrids ha

Interspecific hybrids are infertile. T

d since the antiquity.

and continue to do so to in order to maintain their existence. *It's a lot of work.*

ot impossible, just a bit awkward.

Keep him in this manner for a few months, leading him about regularly by his halter,

people must bring them into being,

Then, on a quiet night, one can lead him to the mare and let him cover her ...

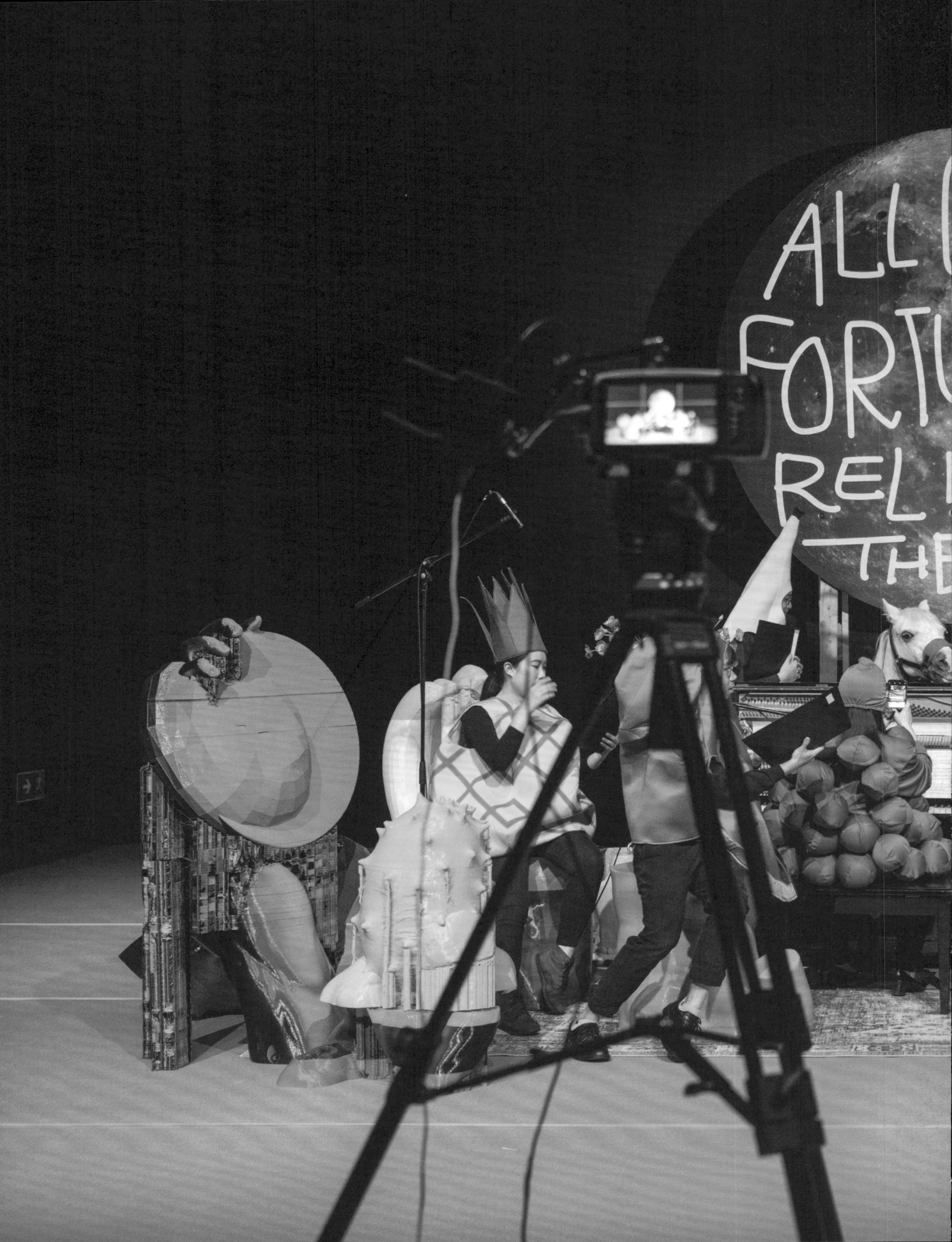
ALL
FORTU
REL
THE

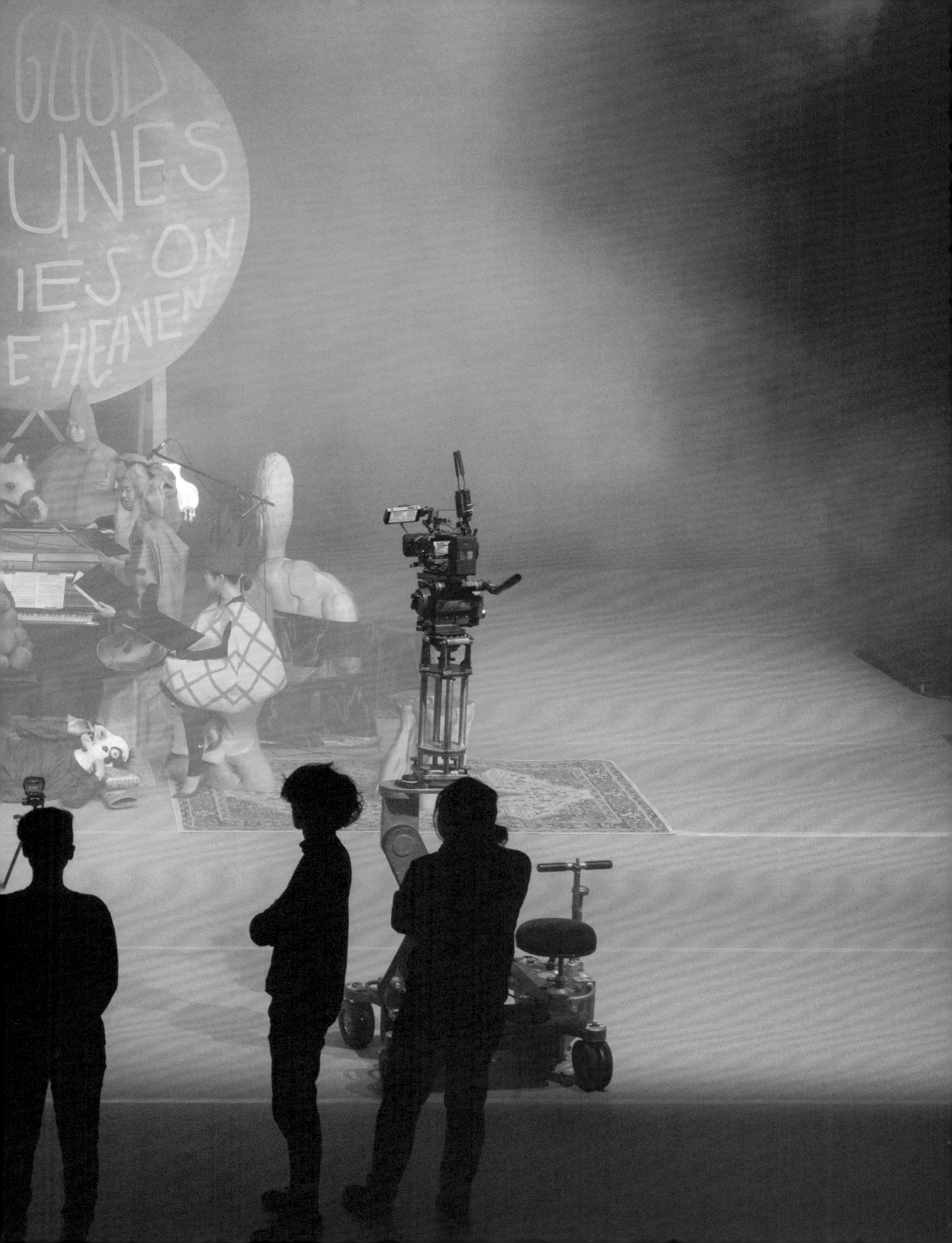
GOOD
UNES
IES ON
E HEAVEN

Exhibition Checklist

WORKS BY SAMSON YOUNG
BORN HONG KONG, 1979

City Garden
2019
C-prints on archival paper, set of 14
Each: 6 1/8 x 10 in. (15.6 x 25.4 cm)
Courtesy of the artist

City Garden (aquarium and cramp school)
2019
C-print, lightbox
30 x 19 3/4 x 4 3/4 in. (76 x 50 x 12 cm)
Courtesy of the artist

Da Da Company
2019
Single-channel video installation with stereo sound,
11:55 min.; slat walls, dropped ceiling, repurposed
office chairs, interactive light system
Courtesy of the artist

The highway is like a lion's mouth
2018
Single-channel video installation with stereo sound,
10:53 min.; CNC-milled foam, carpet, Styrofoam
Courtesy of the artist

Houses of Tomorrow
2019
Single-channel video installation with 8-channel
sound, 20 min.; CNC-milled foam sculpture,
3D-printed PLA
Courtesy of the artist

Line follower
2019
Electronics and sensor with custom software, spray
paint on carpet, soft pastel on 3D-printed PLA
Dimensions variable
Courtesy of the artist

*My car makes noises (show me the bones under the
floor in your room)*
2018
Ink, colored pencil, and pastel on paper
11 3/4 x 8 1/4 in. (30 x 21 cm)
Collection of Tommy Lo

*My car makes noises 6 (a pencil pusher with the
pencil pusher blues)*
2018
Ink, colored pencil, and soft pastel on paper
11 3/4 x 8 1/4 in. (30 x 21 cm)
Courtesy of William Lim, Living Collection

My car makes noises 7 (angry birds)
2018
Ink, colored pencil, and soft pastel on paper
11 3/4 x 8 1/4 in. (30 x 21 cm)
Private Collection, Courtesy of Edouard Malingue
Gallery

My car makes noises 9 (bllgh blllgggh blllllgggghh)
2018
Ink pen, colored pencil, and soft pastel on paper
11 3/4 x 8 1/4 in. (30 x 21 cm)
Private Collection, Courtesy of Edouard Malingue
Gallery

My car makes noises 16 (thud)
2018
Ink pen, colored pencil, and soft pastel on paper
11 3/4 x 8 1/4 in. (30 x 21 cm)
Private Collection, Courtesy of Edouard Malingue
Gallery

My car makes noises 17 (squealing is very linear)
2018
Ink, colored pencil, and soft pastel on paper
11 3/4 x 8 1/4 in. (30 x 21 cm)
Courtesy of William Lim, Living Collection

Support structures series
2019
3D-printed PLA, resin
Dimensions variable
Courtesy of the artist

To Whom It May Concern series
2019
Ink on paper, set of four
Each: 8 1/4 x 11 3/4 in. (21 x 29.8 cm)
Courtesy of the artist

*The world falls apart into facts #2 (The Dream Seller
by E. Markham Lee as performed by the Chinese
University of Hong Kong Chorus)*
2019
Single-channel video with stereo sound, 8 min.
Courtesy of the Artist

WORKS BY OTHER ARTISTS

Karel Lodr
Austro-Hungarian/Czech, 1915–1998
Collective Living (Kolektivni Bydleni 1)
1935
Pen and ink, black wash, pencil, colored pencil,
crayon, clipped and pasted halftone photographs and
architectural photostat, cut sheets of colored paper
on card stock
23 1/2 x 39 in. (59.7 x 99.1 cm)
Purchase, The Paul and Miriam Kirkley Fund for
Acquisitions, Smart Museum of Art, The University of
Chicago

Lou Stoumen
American, 1917–1991
Unemployed Men Times Square, NYC
1940
Gelatin silver print
11 x 14 in. (27.6 x 35.4 cm)
Gift of the Estate of Lester and Betty Guttman, Smart
Museum of Art, The University of Chicago

ARCHIVAL MATERIALS

**ALEXANDER WON CUMYOW'S PERSONAL
CORRESPONDENCE AND RELATED EPHEMERA,
COURTESY OF RARE BOOKS AND SPECIAL
COLLECTIONS, THE UNIVERSITY OF BRITISH
COLUMBIA, VANCOUVER**

Chinese Immigration Service registration card for
Won Alexander Cumyow, issued by the Department of
Immigration and Colonization, Dominion of Canada,
1924
4 3/4 x 7 in. (12.1 x 18 cm)

Envelope and letter addressed to Alexander Won
Cumyow from the Governor General's Secretary on
behalf of the Association of Canada, Vancouver,
acknowledging the receipt of his petition,
February 28, 1901
Envelope: 4 x 8 7/8 in. (10 x 22.5 cm);
Letter: 12 1/2 x 8 1/4 in. (32 x 20 cm)

Letter addressed to Alexander Won Cumyow from
the Deputy Provincial Secretary, British Columbia,
requesting that he substantiate his status as a British
subject, April 11, 1901
13 x 8 1/4 in. (33.5 x 21 cm)

Supper menu in honor of Kang Yuwei, Executive
Committee of the Chinese Empire Reform Association
of Canada, Vancouver, 1904
6 x 8 1/4 in. (15.8 x 21 cm)

**PUBLICATIONS PRODUCED FOR THE CENTURY
OF PROGRESS INTERNATIONAL EXPOSITION,
CHICAGO, 1933–34, COURTESY OF SPECIAL
COLLECTIONS RESEARCH CENTER, UNIVERSITY
OF CHICAGO LIBRARY**

*All-Wood Exhibit House: The Lumber Industries at a
Century of Progress*
Booklet published by National Lumber Manufacturers
Association, 1934
9 1/8 x 6 in. (23.1 x 15.2 cm)

The Altar of the Green Jade Pagoda
Booklet compiled by Julean Arnold with Chang Wenti,
1933
9 x 6 1/4 in. (23 x 15.9 cm)

Beauty at the Fair
Brochure published by Daggett & Ramsdell, c. 1934
3 1/4 x 4 3/4 in. (8.4 x 12 cm)

*Century of Progress Recipes for Royal Desserts
and Other Tempting Suggestions for Serving Royal
Quick Setting Gelatin, Royal Chocolate & Royal
Vanilla Puddings*
Brochure published by Standard Brands, Inc., 1934
8 1/4 x 5 in. (22 x 12.8 cm)

*The Century of Progress Sunlight House, the Last
Word in Home Satisfaction: The All-Lumber House by
the Lumber Industry of the U.S.A.*
Booklet published by National Lumber Manufacturers
Association, 1933
11 1/2 x 8 1/2 in. (29.3 x 21.8 cm)

*The Chinese Lama Temple, Potala of Jehol: Exhibition
of Historical and Ethnographical Collections Made
by Dr. Gosta Montell, Member of Dr. Sven Hedin's
Expeditions and Donated by Vincent Bendix*
Booklet published by R. R. Donnelly & Sons Co., 1932
9 1/4 x 6 1/4 in. (23.7 x 16 cm)

Chrysler Motors Invites You and Your Friends to Visit Chrysler Motors at a Century of Progress and See the Extraordinary Engineering Features of Plymouth, Dodge, De Soto and Chrysler Cars Dramatized in Thrilling Demonstrations of Quality and Performance
Brochure published by Chrysler Corporation, 1934
11 x 16 3/4 in. (28 x 43 cm), unfolded

Cleanliness Thru the Ages
Booklet published by Old Dutch Cleanser, 1933
8 3/4 x 6 in. (22.3 x 15.1 cm)

Coffee . . . Vacuum Packed in Glass: The Onlzed Method
Brochure published by Owens-Illinois Glass Company, 1933
9 x 6 in. (22.9 x 15.3 cm)

Color Beauties of a Century of Progress, Chicago, 1933
Brochure published by Exposition Publications and Novelties, Inc., 1933
6 1/4 x 8 1/4 in. (16.1 x 21 cm)

Control Weight Safely with Fresh Milk: Diets for Reducing and Gaining Weight
Brochure published by the Milk Foundation, Inc., c. 1933
3 x 3 1/16 in. (7.6 x 7.8 cm)

Crane Bathrooms in Model Homes at Century of Progress
Brochure published by the Crane Company, 1934
6 1/2 x 7 in. (16 x 17.8 cm)

Dairy Products Build Superior People
Booklet published for the Century Dairy Exhibit, Inc., 1933
10 1/4 x 8 1/2 in. (27.5 x 21.6 cm)

Diet, Dentistry, Dentifrice: Souvenir of the three "D" Oral Educational Exhibit
Brochure published by the Iodent Chemical Company, 1933
6 7/8 x 5 1/2 in. (17.5 x 13.8 cm)

Dodge "Show-Down" Score Card: The Modern Way to Judge Motor Car Value
Brochure published by Dodge Brothers, 1934
8 x 20 in. (21 x 51 cm), unfolded

Durkee Famous Foods Recipes
Booklet published by Durkee Famous Foods, 1933
4 5/16 x 6 1/8 in. (10.9 x 15.5 cm)

Durkee Famous Foods Recipes
Booklet published by Durkee Famous Foods, 1934
5 3/8 x 4 3/4 in. (13.7 x 12.1 cm)

"Endless Chain of Cars Moving in a Tower of Glass"
Postcard published by Nash Motors Company, c. 1933
5 1/2 x 3 9/16 in. (14 x 9 cm)

The Florida Tropical Home at a Century of Progress
Booklet published by Kuhne Galleries, 1933
11 1/2 x 8 1/4 in. (29.2 x 20.9 cm)

General Motors Building: A Century of Progress
Brochure published by General Motors Company, 1933
8 3/4 x 5 7/8 in. (22 x 15 cm)

Good Housekeeping Sponsors a Modern Wonder at a Century of Progress
Brochure published by *Good Housekeeping* magazine, 1933
14 1/2 x 10 1/8 in. (37 x 25.7 cm)

A House of Rostone at a Century of Progress
Brochure published by Rostone, Inc., 1933
5 3/8 x 8 1/2 in. (13.6 x 21.5 cm)

House of Tomorrow: America's First Glass House
Brochure published by Century Homes, Inc., 1933
9 1/2 x 6 3/4 in. (24.2 x 17.1 cm)

Hupmobile Aerodynamic
Booklet published by Hupp Motor Car Company, 1934
13 x 12 in. (33 x 31 cm)

The Making of a Motor Car
Souvenir guidebook published by General Motors Company, 1933
8 3/4 x 5 1/2 in. (22 x 14 cm)

Meat Curing Made Easy and a New Way to Make Sausage
Booklet published by the Morton Salt Company, c. 1933
10 7/8 x 8 1/2 in. (27.6 x 21.5 cm)

Modern Bathrooms and Kitchens
Booklet published by Kohler Company, 1933
9 x 6 1/8 in. (22.9 x 15.5 cm)

The Money of the World: Interesting Facts About the Principal Nations of the World and Their Coinage
Booklet published by the National Cash Register Company, 1933
6 1/2 x 4 1/2 in. (16.1 x 11.8 cm)

1933 A Century Of Progress Chicago: Armco-Ferro Porcelain Enameled House Built By Ferro Enamel Corporation and American Rolling Mill Company
Brochure published by the Ferro Enamel Corporation, 1933
6 1/2 x 3 1/2 in. (16 x 8.8 cm)

Official Pictures of a Century of Progress Exposition: Photographs by Kaufmann & Fabry Co., Official Photographers
Booklet published by the R. H. Donnelley Corporation, 1933
10 x 7 in. (25.5 x 17.9 cm)

100 Years of Progress in Family Finance
Brochure published by the Household Finance Corporation, 1933
9 x 6 in. (23 x 15.3 cm)

1000 B.C. versus 1934 A.D.
Brochure published by Health-o-Meter Company, 1934
6 x 3 1/2 in. (15.5 x 8.8 cm)

Own a Ford Car Through UCC
Brochure published by Universal Credit Company, 1934
7 x 5 in. (18 x 13 cm)

Progress in Infant Feeding
Booklet published by Gerber Products Company, 1933
7 x 5 in. (17.8 x 12.6 cm)

The Progress of Manchuria
Brochure published by South Manchuria Railway, 1933
17 7/8 x 11 7/8 in. (45.4 x 30.2 cm)

Research at a Century of Progress
Brochure published by General Motors Company, 1933
6 3/4 x 4 in. (17 x 10 cm)

Roads of the World
Brochure published by Ford Motor Company, 1934
6 x 13 3/4 in. (16 x 35 cm), unfolded

Sears is Seeking America's Most Beautiful Baby
Brochure published by Sears, Roebuck and Company, 1934
6 1/2 x 3 1/2 in. (16.3 x 9.1 cm)

Simplified Hospitality with Servel Hermetic
Booklet published by Servel Sales, Inc., c. 1932
9 x 6 in. (22.9 x 15.3 cm)

Sloane's House of Today at the Century of Progress Exposition, Chicago: Traditional Charm in the Modern Manner
Booklet published by W. & J. Sloane, 1933
8 1/2 x 11 in. (21.6 x 28.1 cm)

Smart Savories from a Century of Progress
Booklet published by Kraft-Phenix Cheese Corporation, 1933
5 1/2 x 3 1/4 in. (14.1 x 8.3 cm)

Souvenir: A Century of Progress International Exhibition
Published by Plymouth Motor Corporation, 1933
5 1/3 x 3 1/2 in. (14 x 9 cm)

Stran-Steel House at a Century of Progress Exhibited in Co-operation with Good Housekeeping
Booklet published by the Stran-Steel Corporation, 1933
11 1/2 x 8 1/2 in. (29.3 x 21.6 cm)

The Super-Safe Home of the Future
Booklet published by the Brick Manufacturers' Association of America, 1933
11 x 8 1/2 in. (28 x 21.5 cm)

Tidewater Red Cypress: "The Wood Eternal"
Booklet published by the Southern Cypress Manufacturers Association, 1933
11 1/2 x 8 1/2 in. (29.1 x 21.5 cm)

Travels of a Rolled Oat: A Momento of the Quaker Oats Company
Brochure published by the Quaker Oats Company, 1934
7 3/8 x 5 3/8 in. (18.8 x 13.7 cm)

A Visit to the General Motors Research Laboratories at A Century of Progress
Brochure published by General Motors Company, 1934
5 x 17 in. (13 x 44 cm), unfolded